CAMBRIDGE STUDIES IN
ANGLO-SAXON ENGLAND

28

ANGLO-SAXON GESTURES AND
THE ROMAN STAGE

CAMBRIDGE STUDIES IN ANGLO-SAXON ENGLAND

Founding general editors
MICHAEL LAPIDGE AND SIMON KEYNES

Current general editors
SIMON KEYNES AND ANDY ORCHARD

Volumes published

ANGLO-SAXON GESTURES
AND
THE ROMAN STAGE

C. R. DODWELL
prepared for publication by Timothy Graham

CAMBRIDGE
UNIVERSITY PRESS

1002860890

PUBLISHED BY THE PRESS SYNDICATE OF THE UNIVERSITY OF CAMBRIDGE
The Pitt Building, Trumpington Street, Cambridge CB2 1RP, United Kingdom

CAMBRIDGE UNIVERSITY PRESS
The Edinburgh Building, Cambridge CB2 2RU, UK   http://www.cup.cam.ac.uk
40 West 20th Street, New York, NY 10011–4211, USA   http://www.cup.org
10 Stamford Road, Oakleigh, Melbourne 3166, Australia

© Cambridge University Press 2000

First published 2000

Printed in the United Kingdom at the University Press, Cambridge

Typeset in Garamond 11/13pt   [CE]

A catalogue record for this book is available from the British Library

Library of Congress cataloguing in publication data
Dodwell, C. R. (Charles Reginald)
Anglo-Saxon gestures and the Roman stage / by C. R. Dodwell;
prepared for publication by Timothy Graham.
p.   cm. – (Cambridge studies in Anglo-Saxon England; 28)
Includes bibliographical references and index.
ISBN 0 521 66188 9 (hardback)
1. Terence – Illustrations. 2. Illuminations of books and manuscripts, Anglo-Saxon. 3.
Illumination of books and manuscripts, Roman. 4. Latin drama (Comedy) – Appreciation
– England. 5. Latin drama (Comedy) – Illustrations. 6. Latin drama (Comedy) –
manuscripts. 7. Terence – Manuscripts. 8. Acting – Rome – History. 9. Art, Anglo-Saxon.
10. Codice Bembino. 11. Gesture in art. 12. Gesture – Rome.
I. Title. II. Series.
PA6768.D63   2000
872′.01– dc21   99–12836 CIP

ISBN 0 521 66188 9 hardback

T

Contents

v

Plates

to Judah's friend Hirah, Gen. XXXVIII.20–1. (By permission of the British Library.)

XXXIII*b*   Claudius B. iv, 49r. A servant receiving Jacob's instructions, Gen. XXXII.13–19. (By permission of the British Library.)

XXXIV   BL Royal 6. B. VIII, 1v. Opening initial of the Prologue of Isidore's *De fide catholica*. (By permission of the British Library.)

XXXV*a*   Rouen, Bibliothèque Municipale, Y. 6 (274), 32v. Joseph at the Nativity. (Copyright: Bibliothèque Municipale, Rouen.)

XXXV*b*   BL Cotton Tiberius C. vi, 11v. Peter at the Washing of the Feet. (By permission of the British Library.)

XXXVI*a*   BN lat. 7899, 74r. Grief: Clinia, *Heauton timorumenos* III, 3. (Copyright: Bibliothèque Nationale de France.)

XXXVI*b*   Claudius B. iv, 10v. The widow of Enos grieves over her husband's dead body, Gen. V.11. (By permission of the British Library.)

XXXVII   Claudius B. iv, 139v. The children of Israel mourn the death of Moses, Deut. XXXIV.8. (By permission of the British Library.)

XXXVIII*a*   Claudius B. iv, 42v. Isaac laments his mistaken blessing of Jacob in place of Esau, Gen. XXVII.30–5. (By permission of the British Library.)

XXXVIII*b*   Claudius B. iv, 54v. Jacob grieves at the sight of Joseph's coat of many colours, Gen. XXXVII.32–4. (By permission of the British Library.)

XXXIX*a–b*   Oxford, Bodleian Library, Junius 11, pp. 34 and 36. Adam and Eve lament their fall, cf. *Genesis* 765–80. (Copyright: The Bodleian Library, Oxford.)

XL*a*   BL Harley 603, 67v. The Israelites lament their sins, cf. Ps. CXXX.3. (By permission of the British Library.)

XL*b*   Harley 603, 70r. The Israelites weep by the rivers of Babylon, Ps. CXXXVI.1. (By permission of the British Library.)

XLI*a*   Harley 603, 72v. The psalmist laments his plight, Ps. CXLI. (By permission of the British Library.)

XLI*b*   Vatican, Reg. lat. 12, 25r. The personified Unrighteousness laments, cf. Ps. VII.11–17. (Copyright: Biblioteca Apostolica Vaticana.)

Foreword

TIMOTHY GRAHAM

This book is the fruit of many years' work and reflection by Reginald Dodwell. It was probably his researches on the Old English illustrated Hexateuch – the manuscript from which many of the examples in the final chapter are drawn, and in the 1974 facsimile publication of which he collaborated – that first drew his attention to the subject here studied. He perceived a strong similarity between gestures portrayed in certain areas of late Anglo-Saxon art and those occurring in the illustrated manuscripts of the plays of Terence, of which the earliest surviving copies are Carolingian, but which ultimately derive from a late antique exemplar that Professor Dodwell believed there were persuasive reasons to date in the third century AD. He realized that the parallels embrace not only the form, but, more significantly, the meaning of the gestures depicted; and that such parallels with the Terence gestures are difficult to find in other areas of medieval European art. He concluded that there must have been present in late Anglo-Saxon England an illustrated copy of the plays of Terence, and that the meaning of the gestures in its illustrations was learned through careful attention to that copy. Since, as he argues in this book, there is a significant likelihood that the illustrations in the original late antique exemplar drew upon their artist's experience of actual stage productions, it is possible to posit a line of continuity between the late Roman stage and the art of the late Anglo-Saxon period.

Professor Dodwell first lectured on the theme of Anglo-Saxon gestures at the Courtauld Institute in the early 1970s, and followed this up with lectures in Manchester and Reading. Several years later, in 1978, he spoke on 'The Illustrated Copies of Terence with Special Reference to Dramatic Gestures' at the Seminar on Topics in Current Research at the University of Manchester. When, in 1988, he received an invitation to deliver the

1989 Ford Lecture at the University of Oxford, he returned to the theme that had captured his attention for so long, and drew his title, 'Anglo-Saxon Attitudes', from Lewis Carroll's well-known phrase in *Alice through the Looking Glass*. Following the Ford Lecture, he received strong encouragement to publish. Over the next years he focused his scholarly activities on the conversion of his lectures into a book into which he incorporated evidence revealed by his researches that it had been impossible to include in the lecture format, while also expanding the scope of his study through new investigations. He wished the book to be published by Cambridge University Press, which had published his first book, *The Canterbury School of Illumination*, in 1954, and was pleased when his proposal was met by the offer to include the book in the series Cambridge Studies in Anglo-Saxon England. At the time of Professor Dodwell's much lamented death in April 1994, the book was complete in its essentials, requiring only the checking of details and the formating of its text to fit with the requirements of the series. Having served as Professor Dodwell's research assistant throughout the 1980s, I was asked by Mrs Sheila Dodwell and by the series editors to carry out this remaining work. It has been my pleasure and my privilege to do so.

Acknowledgements

In the course of his researches on gestures in the Terence manuscripts and in Anglo-Saxon art, Reginald Dodwell corresponded with numerous scholars, librarians and museum keepers, seeking their reaction to his views and their expert advice in specific areas. Several of his correspondents had attended his lectures and generously responded with helpful observations indicating further lines of investigation for him to pursue. Reginald Dodwell would surely have wished the help of all these individuals to be acknowledged. I record here the names of those known to me: François Avril, David Bain, Bruce Barker-Benfield, M. L. Bierbrier, Bernhard Bischoff, Manfred Bräude, Peter Brown, David Clarke, Gillian Evans, John N. Grant, K. R. Gray, Jennifer Harris, J. W. Hayes, Harry Jocelyn, Catherine Johns, Arthur Johnston, George Kerferd, Otto Kurz, Peter Lasko, Roger Ling, D. Michaelides, Florentine Mütherich, Gale Owen-Crocker, Margaret Packer, Kenneth Painter, David Palmer, Michael Reeve, Richard Schofield, Leah Scragg, Elizabeth Sears, Katherine Dunbabin Slater, Jocelyn Toynbee, Piers Tyrrell and Inge Wintzer. May those whose names have been inadvertently omitted from this list know that their contribution also has been warmly appreciated.

The inclusion of so many illustrations in this book would have been impossible without the help of a generous Publication Subvention from the British Academy, here gratefully acknowledged. The illustrations are published with the permission of the Ny Carlsberg Glyptotek, Copenhagen; the Ministry of Culture, Hellenic Republic; the Augustinian Sisters, Ince Blundell Hall, Liverpool; the Embassy of Greece, London; the British Library, London; the Biblioteca Ambrosiana, Milan; the Metropolitan Museum of Art, New York; the Bodleian Library, Oxford; the Bibliothèque Nationale de France, Paris; the Bibliothèque Municipale, Rouen; the Musée National du Bardo, Tunis; the Biblioteca Apostolica Vaticana; the Monumenti, Musei e Gallerie Pontificie, Vatican City; the Kunsthistorisches Museum, Vienna; and the Musées de Vienne.

TIMOTHY GRAHAM
Visiting International Scholar
The Medieval Institute, Western Michigan University

Abbreviations

BL	London, British Library
BN	Paris, Bibliothèque Nationale de France
C	Vatican City, Biblioteca Apostolica Vaticana, Vat. lat. 3868
CCCC	Corpus Christi College, Cambridge
EEMF	Early English Manuscripts in Facsimile
EETS	Early English Text Society
F	Milan, Biblioteca Ambrosiana, S.P. 4 bis (formerly H 75 inf.)
J&M	L. W. Jones and C. R. Morey, *The Miniatures of the Manuscripts of Terence prior to the Thirteenth Century*, 2 vols. (Princeton, [1931])
MGH	Monumenta Germaniae Historica
P	Paris, Bibliothèque Nationale de France, lat. 7899
PL	Patrologia Latina, ed. J.-P. Migne, 221 vols. (Paris, 1844–64)
RS	Rolls Series
Vatican	Vatican City, Biblioteca Apostolica Vaticana

1

The Vatican Terence and its model

'The art of gesture', says Beare in his book on *The Roman Stage*, 'was carried in ancient times to a height which we can scarcely comprehend.'[1]

All scholars would agree on the importance of gestures to the Roman actor. The fact that he had to project his voice over the length and breadth of an auditorium in a theatre which was vast in size and was in the open air, meant that he could not indicate the age, sex, class or mood of the character he was portraying by any modulation of speech. In fact, he declaimed his words and did so, moreover, to the accompaniment of a flute. Nor could he use facial expressions to reveal feelings or moods, since his face was hidden behind a mask. This meant that he had to depend to a very considerable extent on gestures. Yet little is known about these – what they were or what they signified. It was a subject that interested a few scholars before the First World War, but it was one that fell out of favour before the beginning of the Second, and the aim of our present study is to take a new look at the subject, using a resource that has been known for a considerable time but which, for reasons that will appear, has been discounted for several decades. We shall attempt to identify the appearance and meanings of a number of the Roman theatrical gestures and later to show how some of them were adopted by artists in Anglo-Saxon England. And, as we shall end in the Middle Ages, so we shall begin there, for we shall initiate our investigation with the consideration of a specific work of art of the Carolingian Renaissance.

The Carolingian Renaissance began in the late eighth century and continued into the late ninth, and one of its characteristics was a pronounced interest in classical literature. Even a prominent church

---

[1] Beare, *The Roman Stage*, p. 183.

1

reformer, sending a letter to an abbot asking him to bring relics of saints back with him from Rome, could append to it a quotation from Ovid's *Ars amatoria*,[2] and the Carolingian writers themselves were looking to Rome for their models. So, Einhard, one of the statesmen of the time, wrote a biography of Charlemagne in imitation of Suetonius' *Vitae Caesarum*,[3] and Carolingian poets, such as Alcuin, Angilbert, Modoin, Hrabanus Maurus, Florus, Paul the Deacon and Sedulius Scotus, based their styles on those of Virgil, Ovid, Horace and Lucan.[4] There was also an occasional interest in classical art, a good example of which is a verse account, written in the style of Ovid by a bishop[5] who was also one of Charlemagne's travelling administrators. Along with other inducements to point his judgement in the right direction, he had been offered at Narbonne a Roman bowl having on it a number of scenes from classical mythology (some of them badly rubbed and difficult to discern), and the detailed description and identifications he gives of them would do credit to any scholar of today.[6] Occasionally, the Carolingian arts themselves displayed close links with those of the classical past. Although not in its original condition, a surviving bronze statuette of a real, or ideal, Carolingian emperor[7] is obviously based on a larger-scale equestrian statue of a Roman emperor, and we have a sketch for a triumphal arch[8] which clearly owes much to the Roman arches of antiquity.

Carolingian miniaturists could occasionally reproduce Roman originals, and do so with such fidelity that their own pictures might easily pass as classical ones. Indeed, if they so wished, historians of late antique art could make use of such Carolingian copies in the same way that historians of Greek art have tried to take advantage of Roman reproductions. A tenth-century Carolingian copy (now lost) of a late classical calendrical manuscript included personifications of the months and other illustrations that are believed to have been virtual duplicates of the fourth-century originals,[9] and the painting of a seated figure, made at a

---

[2] This was Alcuin; see Duemmler, *Epistolae Karolini aevi* II, 141.

[3] For which see Pertz and Waitz, *Einhardi vita Karoli Magni*.

[4] See Raby, *A History of Secular Latin Poetry* I, ch. V *passim*, and Raby, *A History of Christian-Latin Poetry*, ch. VI *passim*.

[5] This was Theodulf.   [6] See Duemmler, *Poetae latini aevi Carolini* I, 498–9.

[7] Hubert, Porcher and Volbach, *Carolingian Art*, pl. 206.

[8] See *ibid.*, pl. 29, for a reconstruction.

[9] The lost Carolingian copy is known from two copies made in the late sixteenth and

studio within Charlemagne's own court circle,[10] is so remarkably antique in style that it has actually been claimed by one distinguished scholar to be itself a late Roman original.[11] Again, the portrayal of Perseus in an astronomical collection at Leiden[12] could easily be mistaken for a classical work of art, while the representation of the head of Eridanus, now in London,[13] is in a style indistinguishable from that of the classical period. Some of this accurate copying resulted in works that I once described as facsimiles,[14] and the most famous, and indeed the most extensive, example of these is a cycle of illustrations of the plays of the second-century BC playwright, Terence, which is now in the Vatican Library (Vat. lat. 3868).[15]

Although his comedies were variously received by his contemporaries – on the one hand, the first performance of one was deserted in favour of such trivial attractions as a boxing match and a tightrope walker,[16] and on the other, the appeal of another was such that it was performed twice in a single day[17] – they were such models of clear and elegant Latin and so perceptive in their comments on the human condition that they came to be highly esteemed by the discerning of almost all succeeding

early seventeenth centuries: Brussels, Bibliothèque Royale, 7524–55, fols. 190–211; and Vatican, Barb. lat. 2154 and Vat. lat. 9135. Stern concluded from his study of these that the Carolingian copy so faithfully reproduced the original that it 'n'a laissé aucune trace dans la tradition des images. Cette copie a dû être l'un de ces manuscrits illustrés dont les dessinateurs reproduisaient trait pour trait leurs modèles antiques.' See Stern, *Le Calendrier de 354*, p. 11; and cf. also Gaspar and Lyna, *Les Principaux Manuscrits à peintures de la Bibliothèque Royale de Belgique* I, no. 1. For a reproduction of one of the illustrations in the sixteenth-century Brussels copy, see Dodwell, *Painting in Europe*, pl. 11.

[10] Brussels, Bibliothèque Royale, 18723.
[11] Swarzenski, 'The Xanten Purple Leaf', esp. pp. 22–3.
[12] Leiden, Universiteitsbibliotheek, Voss. Lat. Qu. 79, 40v; see Bullough, *The Age of Charlemagne*, pl. 46.
[13] BL Harley 647, 10v; see Dodwell, *Painting in Europe*, pl. 12, and Dodwell, *Pictorial Arts*, pl. 34.
[14] *Painting in Europe*, p. 23.
[15] The complete manuscript is reproduced in photographic facsimile in Jachmann, *Terentius. Codex Vaticanus latinus 3868*.
[16] This is stated in the two Prologues of *Hecyra*: *Prologus (I)* 1–5 and *Prologus (II)* 25–8. The same play later lost its audience to the counter-attraction of a gladiatorial show: *Prologus (II)* 39–42.
[17] Suetonius says this of *Eunuchus*. See Radice, *Terence: the Comedies*, Appendix A, p. 390.

generations; not least by those of the Middle Ages, who have bequeathed to us the earliest surviving copies of his complete works. Some are illustrated, and all students of the subject are indebted to Jones and Morey for publishing a corpus of all the related miniatures made before the thirteenth century.[18] Although, as we shall see in a later chapter, we shall find another illustrated Terence, now in Paris, to be of considerable importance, it is to the one in the Vatican that we shall direct most of our attention in this study.

THE ARCHETYPE OF THE VATICAN TERENCE

According to the generally accepted view of Bischoff,[19] the Vatican Terence was made at Corvey, although it probably later passed to the parent house of Corbie from which Corvey was colonized. He dates it to the period 820–30.[20] It has the unusual distinction for a Carolingian manuscript of providing the name of the scribe (Hrodgarius) and of one of the three artists (Adelricus), who gives us his name on fol. 3r, associating with it a prayer for God's mercy. (It was by no means unusual for the scribe of a theological work in the Middle Ages to associate his endeavours with a petition to God, yet, curious as it may seem to us today that an artist should suppose that God would look favourably on a secular and pagan work, this may have something to tell us about attitudes to Terence within medieval monasteries.) The script is Carolingian but the pictures – and, excluding prefatory material, there are no less than 144 of these – are accepted as being remarkably accurate copies of classical originals, characteristic comments being that the cycle represents an 'unusually careful rendition of an antique model',[21] and that it is 'a most faithful copy' of a late classical original.[22] No one will dispute that the pictures are so close to their prototypes that they can be virtually treated as Roman works themselves, although the date of those prototypes is very much a matter of controversy. Indeed, in tracing the numerous scholarly

---

[18] Jones and Morey, *The Miniatures of the Manuscripts of Terence*.

[19] Bischoff, 'Hadoardus and the Manuscripts of Classical Authors from Corbie', p. 54 n. 3. Koehler and Mütherich, however, prefer to leave open the question of the place of origin of the manuscript: see *Die karolingischen Miniaturen* IV, 76.

[20] Bischoff, *ibid.*   [21] J&M II, 36.

[22] Weitzmann, *Late Antique and Early Christian Book Illumination*, p. 13.

pronouncements about the archetype of the Vatican Terence, we are sometimes reminded of the remark made by one of the lawyers in Terence's play *Phormio* that 'quot homines tot sententiae'.[23]

If we leave on one side the wildly differing dates suggested in the nineteenth century, we can point to the fact that, in the first two decades of the twentieth, proposals varied from the first century BC, which had the support of an art historian as eminent as Carl Robert,[24] to the fifth or sixth century AD put forward by Engelhardt.[25] Later, in 1924, Jachmann favoured the end of the third or beginning of the fourth century, chiefly on literary evidence,[26] and in the following year, on art-historical data, Rodenwaldt sought to prove that the pictures could not have been made before the second half of the fourth century.[27] In 1939, Bieber suggested a date in the fourth or fifth century,[28] and in the same year, Byvanck more positively, but on remarkably limited evidence, declared for the years 410–20.[29] In 1945, Bethe noted similarities with works of the first century,[30] and since then, Weitzmann and Koehler and Mütherich have declared for the fifth century.[31] These are not all the opinions given, and I have left to the last the most influential of all, which was that of Jones and Morey.

In 1931, they argued for a date in 'the latter part of the fifth century or even *c.* 500',[32] basing their conclusions partly on an art-historical

---

[23] 'There are as many opinions as there are men to give them' (*Phormio* 454).

[24] Robert, *Die Masken der neueren attischen Komoedie*, pp. 87–108, esp. p. 108.

[25] Engelhardt, *Die Illustrationen der Terenzhandschriften*, esp. pp. 57 and 90–1.

[26] Jachmann, *Die Geschichte des Terenztextes*, p. 119.

[27] Rodenwaldt, 'Cortinae', esp. pp. 47–9.

[28] Bieber, *The History of the Greek and Roman Theater*, p. 153.

[29] Byvanck, 'Das Vorbild der Terenzillustrationen', p. 135: 'Man wird ihn also etwa zwischen 410 und 420 datieren dürfen.'

[30] Bethe, *Buch und Bild im Altertum*, p. 61, where he compares the Terence illustrations with the wall-paintings of Pompeii and Herculaneum. Bethe's book was posthumously edited by E. Kirsten.

[31] Weitzmann, *Late Antique and Early Christian Book Illumination*, p. 13; Koehler and Mütherich, *Die karolingischen Miniaturen* IV, 75.

[32] J&M II, 45. Earlier, Morey had said much the same in 'I miniatori del Terenzio illustrato della Biblioteca Vaticana', pp. 50–3. A few pages on (p. 58) Morey remarks (as he does in his later publication) that the cylindrical headgear worn by Thraso in *Eunuchus* is first found used by the military in the porphyry imperial statuettes of St Mark's, Venice. However, it was already in use by civilians in the second century AD as we see from the second-century funeral stele of a merchant from Aquileia in which the

analysis (which, incidentally, led them to claim that the artist was 'one schooled in the Greco-Asiatic manner, and presumably a Greek'),[33] and partly on a textual criterion, namely on the fifth-century date that Craig had earlier proposed for Calliopius,[34] the recensionist of the version of the text to which belong all the surviving medieval manuscripts of Terence, including the illustrated ones. They were here influenced by the view of Jachmann, which had won general acceptance, that the illustrations had been created for a branch of the textual tradition designated as γ, which itself derived from the Calliopian recension. However, in recent years Grant has argued that anomalies in the relationship between the miniatures and the Calliopian recension and its γ branch indicate that the illustrations were created for a non-Calliopian manuscript, and subsequently imported into the γ branch at an undetermined point in its development.[35] If this is correct, it would mean that the date of origin of the illustrations need not be later than that of Calliopius, which itself remains a matter of debate. In any event, it is the view of the present writer that there is enough art-historical evidence to establish the date of the miniatures in the third century AD. Two of the indications for this are to be found in the very first picture (pl. I).

Dates of hair-styles, etc.

This is an author 'portrait' – a portrayal of Terence[36] – in a format which follows a familiar classical formula going back to embossed or painted shields described by Pliny[37] and known as the *imago clipeata*,[38] in which a bust is presented in a roundel held by two supporters. These could either be centaurs, as on the Dionysiac sarcophagi,[39] or winged Victories, as on

latter is shown wearing a fez-like hat: see Bianchi Bandinelli, *Rome: the Late Empire*, pl. 105. Webster, *Monuments Illustrating New Comedy*, p. 210, thinks that it may be 'a restylization of the Macedonian *causia*'.

[33] J&M II, 40. On p. 198, they say that he was 'probably a Greek'.

[34] *Ibid.*, p. 200.   [35] Grant, *Studies in the Textual Tradition of Terence*, p. 21.

[36] A good colour reproduction of it forms the frontispiece of J&M I; see also Dodwell, *Pictorial Arts*, pl. 33.

[37] *Naturalis historia* XXXV.iii.4 (ed. Mayhoff V, 232).

[38] The standard work on which is now Winkes, *Clipeata imago*.

[39] Matz, *Die dionysischen Sarkophage* IV, pls. 286 (nos. 268 and 269), 290 (nos. 270 and 272) and 291 (nos. 267 and 273).

the sarcophagus of the Seasons in Washington,[40] or winged Cupids, as on a sarcophagus from Roman Gaul,[41] although appropriately enough in the Terence, the supporters are two actors, who hold up a placard resting on a small column and with a portrayal of Terence on it. This is clearly an imagined likeness, and one which no doubt reflected the trends in portraiture of the day. Ovid has an amused reference to the rapidly changing fashions of ladies' coiffures (*Ars amatoria* III.152), but the hair-styles of men in the Roman period also had their vogues. They were presumably set by the ruling class, especially the emperors, and an examination of these will be a positive help in any dating procedures. With this in mind, we might consider those of the third century AD.

The century began with an emperor who boasted flowing locks, which are shown in surviving representations of him. He was Septimius Severus (193–211).[42] After the much reduced style of his immediate successor, Caracalla (211–17),[43] however, the others favoured quite different styles and opted for a very much shorter haircut, which was perhaps better suited to the new race of soldier-emperors – those raised from the army to the purple. Contemporary likenesses show that they set a fashion that dominated the rest of the first half of the third century: one which was a gentler form of the style that we would today describe as *en brosse* – very short without being shaven, and with a pronounced peak at the front. We see it first taken up by Macrinus (217–18),[44] and – after the rule of the boy-emperor, Elagabalus (218–22)[45] – resumed in turn by Alexander Severus (222–35),[46] Maximinus Thrax (235–8),[47] Gordian III (238–44)[48]

---

[40] Bianchi Bandinelli, *Rome: the Late Empire*, pl. 72.

[41] Espérandieu, *Recueil général des bas-reliefs* II, pl. on p. 117 (no. 1057).

[42] Bianchi Bandinelli, *Rome: the Late Empire*, pls. 64 and 247.

[43] See Wiggers and Wegner, *Caracalla, Geta, Plautilla*, pp. 9–92 and pls. 1–23; and Hekler, *Greek & Roman Portraits*, pl. 290.

[44] See Wiggers and Wegner, *Caracalla, Geta, Plautilla*, pp. 131–40 and pls. 30–3; and Poulsen, *Les Portraits romains* II, 138 (no. 138) and pls. CCXX–CCXXI.

[45] See Wiggers and Wegner, *Caracalla, Geta, Plautilla*, pp. 146–52 and pls. 38–41; and Kent, *Roman Coins*, pl. 117 (nos. 414–15).

[46] See Wiggers and Wegner, *Caracalla, Geta, Plautilla*, pp. 177–99 and pls. 44–56a and 65a.

[47] *Ibid.*, pp. 223–8 and pls. 64b, 66–9, 70b and 72f; and Hekler, *Greek & Roman Portraits*, pl. 291a.

[48] See Wegner, *Gordianus III. bis Carinus*, pp. 13–29 and pls. 1–9; and Hekler, *Greek & Roman Portraits*, pl. 292. A good comparison with the portrait of Philip can be made

7

and Philip the Arab (244–9).[49] With the turn of the half-century, this particular style went out of fashion and both Decius (249–51)[50] and Trebonianus (251–3)[51] had quite different, heavily cropped hair, while their successors, Gallienus (253–68)[52] and Claudius II (268–70),[53] had longish hair. Within a specific period, then – from *c.* 217 to *c.* 249 – there was a well defined style – the *en brosse* one – and the significance of this is that the Terence portrayal shows him following this fashion. During the course of its vogue, there were small variations, although both Gordian III and Philip the Arab had exactly the same haircut and we may note that Terence's is remarkably similar to theirs. This we shall see if we compare a marble portrait-bust of Philip in the Vatican (pl. II*a*) with the representation of Terence in the Vatican manuscript (pl. II*b*). What is more, Philip also had a beard and sideburns resembling those of Terence, although this comes out less clearly in the life-size marble head of him that we illustrate in order to show him full-face as in the miniature than in a profile likeness on a silver medallion now in the Bibliothèque Nationale de France.[54] On the basis of these comparisons, we might reasonably suppose that the picture of Terence was made in the first half of the third century and probably in its second quarter.[55]

In the full perspective of history, fashions can, of course, recur and it is therefore important to see that the suggested dating of our Terence picture by reference to the hair-style of Philip the Arab is given some

from the side-by-side reproductions in Van der Meer and Mohrmann, *Atlas of the Early Christian World*, figs. 25 and 26.

[49] See Wegner, *Gordianus III. bis Carinus*, pp. 30–41 and pls. 10–14; and Hekler, *Greek & Roman Portraits*, pl. 293.

[50] See Wegner, *Gordianus III. bis Carinus*, pp. 63–9 and pls. 26–8; and Bianchi Bandinelli, *Rome: the Late Empire*, pl. 8.

[51] See Wegner, *Gordianus III. bis Carinus*, pp. 83–91 and pls. 29 and 34–5. The identification of the New York statue as Trebonianus is here rejected by Wegner (pp. 89–90), but it is tentatively accepted by Wood, *Roman Portrait Sculpture*, pp. 43–5. See also Bianchi Bandinelli, *Rome: the Late Empire*, pl. 21.

[52] See Wegner, *Gordianus III. bis Carinus*, pp. 106–20 and pls. 40–7; and Hekler, *Greek & Roman Portraits*, pl. 298.

[53] See Wegner, *Gordianus III. bis Carinus*, pp. 135–8 and pl. 52; and Bianchi Bandinelli, *Rome: the Late Empire*, pl. 390.

[54] BN, Cabinet des Médailles, no. 88; see Bianchi Bandinelli, *Rome: the Late Empire*, pl. 382.

[55] We find the Terence style also in the portrayal of Macrinus cited above, but I presume that, at this stage, it had not yet become a fashion.

support when we compare the facial expressions of playwright and emperor.

Before the third century AD, the demeanour and expression of the sitter had tended to be conventionalized or ritualized, by which I mean that they were intended to indicate a frame of mind considered appropriate for the profession or status of the sitter. So, representations of poets had shown them projecting feelings or taking up postures that were considered proper for literary figures. As early as *c.* 380 BC, therefore, a figure, thought to be that of Aristophanes, was represented in meditation before theatrical masks,[56] as was Menander much later. The painting of the latter in the House of Menander at Pompeii shows him in a contemplative mood,[57] and a poet in the mosaics of Sousse[58] is characterized in the same way. The famous portrayal of Virgil, also at Sousse,[59] presents him, too, with the air and posture appropriate for poets: namely looking outwards, as if for inspiration, as he sits between two Muses, a scroll containing an extract from the *Æneid* on his lap. There is nothing as stereotyped as this about the image of Terence. He is simply presented as a human being with ordinary human feelings and, indeed, is made to look quite lugubrious, like a sculpted head made a few years earlier and described by Vagn Poulsen as a 'portrait d'un homme mélancolique'.[60] The same is true of the portrait of Philip the Arab in the sense that his expression is not one that the world would associate with a powerful emperor but rather that of a human being with all his strengths and weaknesses. Hekler, indeed, sees chiefly his weaknesses and claims that the 'false look of the eyes and the choleric expression tell us much more of the Emperor's disposition than do the scanty records of the texts'.[61] He claims that the period when the inner feelings of a man could be exposed in this way seems to bridge the years between *c.* 215 and *c.* 250,[62] and he contrasts the portrayals made then with 'the nerveless refinement of the Antonine portraits' that came before, and also with the anti-individual,

---

[56] Bieber, *The History of the Greek and Roman Theater*, fig. 201.

[57] Maiuri, *La Casa del Menandro* I, frontispiece and pp. 106–21, and II, pl. XII.

[58] Dunbabin, *The Mosaics of Roman North Africa*, fig. 131.   [59] *Ibid.*, fig. 130.

[60] Poulsen, *Les Portraits romains* II, 178 (no. 181) and pls. CCXCIII–CCXCIV.

[61] Hekler, *Greek & Roman Portraits*, p. xl.

[62] *Ibid.* Hekler actually says from the bust of Caracalla (211–17) to *c.* 250. For the continuing influence of the images of Caracalla on those of his successors see Wood, *Roman Portrait Sculpture*, pp. 27–48.

rigidly symmetrical portraits that came after.[63] Certainly, as the third quarter of the century began, so portraitists dropped the idea of revealing the human qualities of their imperial sitters and chose instead to present them as the recipients of divine inspiration.[64]

It is not only the image of Terence, but also the depiction of the actors who hold the placard on which it is painted, that offers evidence of a third-century date and we can see this if we compare them to the carvings on a small sarcophagus in the Ince Blundell collection of the Merseyside Museums.[65] Its lid is ornamented with six stage masks. On the two ends are depicted a comic and a tragic mask, each on a table. The main carvings, on the front, present us with two figures standing on either side of a central door and gesturing towards it. They are dressed as actors, and behind each is a flute-player playing his instrument to accompany them. Clearly, the sarcophagus was intended for the remains of someone associated with the theatre, perhaps a writer, and if we compare the left-hand figure here (pl. III*a*) with the left-hand figure in the miniature (pl. III*b*), we shall see some close resemblances, as Webster has already noted.[66] There is, in each, exactly the same positioning of the right arm, and surprisingly enough, exactly the same concealment of the left arm behind the back so that it is lost to view below the elbow. There is also the same backward inclined stance of the body and the same type of chiton. In each, this falls down to the ankles, is decorated near the hem, is bunched up over the stomach, and is gathered at the waist with a sash which falls in folds at the back. Each chiton, furthermore, is decorated with a medallion on the chest. These comparisons are very close indeed, and difficult to reconcile with the remark of Jones and Morey that the style of the Terence miniatures is 'wholly un-Latin'.[67] Webster dates the sarcophagus between 250 and 300.[68]

One very unusual feature of the Vatican manuscript is that, before the texts of five of the six plays, there is an illustration in which the various masks that will be required by the different actors are displayed on

---

[63] Hekler, *Greek & Roman Portraits*, pp. xl–xli.

[64] Bianchi Bandinelli, *Rome: the Late Empire*, p. 27.

[65] Ashmole, *Catalogue of the Ancient Marbles at Ince Blundell Hall*, p. 89 (no. 232) and pl. 50. We should, nevertheless, note that doubts have been cast on the authenticity of this sarcophagus by Koch and Sichtermann, *Römische Sarkophage*, p. 123.

[66] Webster, *Monuments Illustrating New Comedy*, IS 50 (p. 218).   [67] J&M II, 198.

[68] Webster, *Monuments Illustrating New Comedy*, p. 219.

shelves. The only parallel that I know to this is a similar exhibition of masks on a shelf in the Maison des Masques at Sousse.[69] Foucher assigned this to the years around 220–30,[70] a dating adopted by Dunbabin in her study of the mosaics of Roman North Africa.[71]

During the middle years of the third century, a particular fashion held sway among the wives of the ruling class. It was one in which a heavy length of hair was looped up from the back of the head to form a flat bun at the top in such a way that the front view simply shows the bun over a central parting. There are good representations of it in surviving heads of the period represented in metal and marble. We can, for example, follow its vogue among women of the imperial families as they are represented in profile on coins. Thus Tranquillina exhibits this style on a coin struck in 242,[72] Otacilia on one of 248,[73] and Etruscilla on two of *c.* 250.[74] Supera is seen following the current mode on a coin of 253,[75] and Salonina on coins of *c.* 255, *c.* 265 and *c.* 267.[76] From this evidence, we might say that the style prevailed between *c.* 242 and *c.* 267. We have already discussed the hair-style of the emperor Philip the Arab, and on the coin of 248 referred to above, we are given a side-view of that of his consort, Otacilia. The same coiffure is even more satisfactorily represented in three dimensions in contemporary sculpted heads of imperial consorts. One such head in the Ny Carlsberg Glyptotek, Copenhagen, is thought by Vagn Poulsen to be that of either Otacilia (244–9) or her predecessor, Tranquillina (238–44), although he finally opts for the latter,[77] a choice favoured by both Wegner[78] and Wood.[79] Another head, also said by two scholars to be that of Tranquillina and now in the British Museum,[80] has the same coiffure. We ourselves have chosen to illustrate as an example of it that on a marble head in the Ny Carlsberg Glyptotek (pl. IV*a*) which

---

[69] Foucher, *La Maison des Masques à Sousse*, p. 14 (fig. 19).   [70] *Ibid.*, p. 59.

[71] Dunbabin, *The Mosaics of Roman North Africa*, p. 271.

[72] Kent, *Roman Coins*, pl. 125 (no. 451).   [73] *Ibid.*, pl. 125 (no. 453).

[74] *Ibid.*, pls. 127 (no. 463) and 128 (no. 468).   [75] *Ibid.*, pl. 129 (no. 478).

[76] *Ibid.*, pls. 130 (no. 482) and 132 (nos. 491 and 492).

[77] See Poulsen, *Les Portraits romains* II, 165–6 (no. 169) and pl. CCLXXI. On the portraits of Otacilia generally see Wegner, *Gordianus III. bis Carinus*, pp. 57–62 and pls. 21*d–f* and 24–5.

[78] *Gordianus III. bis Carinus*, p. 54.   [79] *Roman Portrait Sculpture*, p. 131.

[80] See Bernoulli, *Die Bildnisse der römischen Kaiser* III, 138–9 and pl. XLIII; and Wegner, *Gordianus III. bis Carinus*, p. 54.

Poulsen believes depicts Salonina[81] although there is no complete agreement about this.[82]

However, such accurate identifications are of less importance to us than the fact that all the scholars concerned would agree with Vagn Poulsen's comment that this is 'une coiffure propre au milieu du IIIème s[iècle]'.[83] This is what chiefly matters to us since it will enable us to give a general date to the three representations of the style which appear on female masks in the displays before the Terence plays. Two of them are to be found on the extreme left of the middle and lowest shelves in the array before *Hecyra*,[84] and a third in the aedicula before *Phormio*.[85] In pl. IV *a* and *b* we compare the first mentioned of these masks with the marble head in the Ny Carlsberg Glyptotek, and if we disregard in the miniature the jewelled adornment of the head and also the straggling tresses at the neck, which were part and parcel of masks of the second and third centuries[86] and led to the hair being taken over the ears, then the resemblance between the two is obvious.

Another female mask in the Terence miniatures can be compared with one represented in a different part of the empire. This is at Vienne, in a floor mosaic discovered during the excavations of 1966 at the Place Saint-Pierre, and now in the Musée Saint-Pierre of the town. It is a large work of art, with a central octagon depicting Hercules and the Nemean lion. This has eight squares around containing depictions of theatrical masks, and a further eight octagons beyond with figures of a boxer and other triumphant athletes, a juxtaposition which ironically reminds one of Terence's complaint that the first production of *Hecyra* was forced off the stage by the rival attraction of a boxing match. There are representations of the seasons at the corners, but it is the athletes who have given the

[81] Poulsen, *Les Portraits romains* II, 173–4 (no. 178) and pls. CCLXXXVII–CCLXXXVIII.

[82] Wegner (*Gordianus III. bis Carinus*, p. 131) disagrees, as does Wood (*Roman Portrait Sculpture*, p. 112).

[83] *Les Portraits romains* II, 173.   [84] Vat. lat. 3868, 65r, J&M I, no. 583.

[85] 77r, J&M I, no. 679.

[86] See, for example, Bieber, *The History of the Greek and Roman Theater*, figs. 802, illustrating a mask from the Lateran mosaic of Herakleitos, and 808, showing a mask from a mosaic of the Villa of Hadrian, now in the Vatican. See also masks 1, 4, 5, 6, 10, 12, 13, 14, 15, 19, 21 and 22 in the Maison des Masques at Sousse illustrated by Foucher, *La Maison des Masques à Sousse*, figs. 88, 91, 92, 93, 97, 99, 100, 101, 102, 106, 108 and 109.

mosaic its name as that of the 'Athlètes vainqueurs'. In his close examination of the decoration, choice of motifs, type of composition, colours and style of the mosaic, Tourrenc has come to the conclusion that it belongs to the first part of the third century, and more particularly, to *c.* 220.[87] Now, this is of interest to us. Of interest because, among the Vienne comic masks, we find exactly the same rolling hair-style (pl. V*a*) that we see represented in masks in the aedicula before *Andria*[88] (pl. V*b*) – another general indication that the Terence pictures belong to the third century.

The male masks also point to the same century and can have close resemblances with a mask pictured in the Menander mosaics at Mytilene.

The excavations at Mytilene, the chief city of Lesbos, which commenced in 1961, uncovered a building whose reception hall was decorated with a large mosaic showing Orpheus surrounded by animals and playing a harp. Its triclinium had portrayals in mosaic of a bust of Thalia, the Muse of poetry, with a comic mask, and of Menander, and also three brief scenes from his comedies, together with a representation of three figures from Plato's *Phaedo*, all made by the same workshop, if not by the same artist. They must have been made before *c.* 300 since there is evidence that the house was destroyed then, and on the basis of their style, iconography, and what is known of the history of the edifice, Charitonides, who made the original discovery, has argued for the end of the third quarter of the third century.[89] He himself remarked on the fact that there were resemblances between the Menander scenes and the Terence miniatures in the Vatican manuscript.[90]

Nevertheless, we would for the moment like to focus attention on the coiffure of the comic mask held by Thalia.[91] In it, the hair, which is schematized into a parallel pattern of line, has a high crown – rather like the close-fitting cloche hats of the 1920s – and then descends over the ears (pl. VI*a*). We find the same in a third-century terracotta statuette from the Athens agora (T 36350) reproduced by Charitonides in his pl.

---

[87] Tourrenc, 'La Mosaïque des Athlètes vainqueurs', pp. 139–41. See also Lancha, *Recueil général des mosaïques de la Gaule* III.2 *(Vienne)*, pp. 58–70 (no. 264) and pls. XI–XX, especially pl. XX (in colour).

[88] 3r, J&M I, no. 7, on the extreme left of the second shelf down.

[89] Charitonides, Kahil and Ginouvès, *Les Mosaïques de la Maison du Ménandre à Mytilène*, p. 12.

[90] *Ibid.*, p. 102.   [91] *Ibid.*, pp. 36–7 and pl. 3 (3).

25 (5), in a third-century statuette warrior also from the agora reproduced by Bieber (her fig. 369*a*) and – very much to the point – in our own illustrations. We instance here the style of Syrus (pl. VI*b*) as seen in the illustration on fol. 56r to Act III, scene 3, v. 364 of *Adelphoe*. The same fashion is given to a mask in mosaic in the Maison des Mois at El Djem (pl. VII*a*) which is attributed to the third century.[92] We can compare this with the hair-dress of a mask in the Terence (pl. VII*b*), the one in the array before the text of *Heauton timorumenos* (fol. 35r) and which is in the top range, second from the left. The vogue is also seen in a terracotta comic mask in the Metropolitan Museum (pl. VIII*a*) which Webster has described as 'one of the not very large group of monuments which attest to the existence of dramatic performances in the third century AD'.[93] He dates it partly on the basis of technique and we may note the resemblance between the hair-style here and that in a mask in our own miniatures: the one in the display before *Hecyra* which is to be found on fol. 65r in the second row down, the second to the left (pl. VIII*b*). The fact is that this was a style that was particular to third-century masks and it is certainly the dominant one in the Terence. Here, we already find seventeen examples of it in the displays of masks prefacing the texts of *Heauton timorumenos*,[94] *Adelphoe*,[95] *Hecyra*[96] and *Phormio*,[97] and numerous other examples of it are presented by the different players acting out the various scenes of all six plays. It makes an appearance in the first three illustrations of *Heauton timorumenos*, being used by the Prologue,[98] by both Chremes and Menedemus in Act I, scene 1,[99] and by Chremes addressing Clitipho in Act I, scene 2,[100] as well as by characters elsewhere.[101] In *Adelphoe*, we find it adopted by practically all the male characters at one or other stage of the play: by the Prologue,[102] by Micio,[103] by Demea,[104] by Ctesipho,[105] by

---

[92] Dunbabin, *The Mosaics of Roman North Africa*, p. 260.

[93] Webster, *Monuments Illustrating New Comedy*, UT 110 (p. 238).

[94] 35r, J&M I, no. 323.   [95] 50v, J&M I, no. 449.   [96] 65r, J&M I, no. 583.

[97] 77r, J&M I, no. 679.   [98] 35v, J&M I, no. 326.   [99] 36v, J&M I, no. 331.

[100] 37v, J&M I, no. 338.

[101] As Clitipho in II, 1 (38r, J&M I, no. 344), and Syrus in IV, 2 (44r, J&M I, no. 392), IV, 6 (46r, J&M I, no. 412) and IV, 7 (46v, J&M I, no. 417), etc.

[102] 51r, J&M I, no. 452.

[103] In IV, 3 (59r, J&M I, no. 520), V, 2 (61v, J&M I, no. 549), etc.

[104] In III, 3 (56r upper, J&M I, no. 496), IV, 3 (59r, J&M I, no. 520), etc.

[105] As in IV, 1 and IV, 2, both on 58r (J&M I, nos. 510 and 515).

Hegio,[106] by Syrus,[107] by Dromo[108] and by Geta.[109] It occurs also in the case of the main characters in *Andria*, Simo,[110] Chremes,[111] Davus[112] and Crito.[113] Laches,[114] Chaerea,[115] Parmeno[116] and Gnatho[117] make use of it in *Eunuchus*, Demipho,[118] Chremes,[119] Antipho,[120] Davus[121] and Geta[122] in *Phormio*, and the Prologue,[123] Laches,[124] Phidippus[125] and Parmeno[126] in *Hecyra*.

In yet another sense, evidence can be produced to show that some of the Terence masks are of the third century, for no less an authority on the subject than Webster avers as much. He tells us quite unequivocally that one of the masks in the aedicula before *Andria*, the one of a wavy-haired old man with a pointed beard which will be worn by Chremes in this play (and by Menedemus in *Heauton timorumenos*, by Hegio in *Adelphoe* and by Dorio in *Phormio*) 'is a third century mask', and he compares it with a terracotta mask from the Athens agora and a marble mask from Ostia.[127] He also says that the pseudo-onkos (the setting of the hair forward over the forehead) that appears, for example, in the illustration of Act IV, scene 5 of *Andria* (fol. 15v) is 'a stylisation which first appears in the second century and is very common in the third', and in this connection, he refers us to the Herakleitos mosaic in the Lateran.[128]

---

[106] As in IV, 3 (59r, J&M I, no. 520).

[107] As in II, 2 (53v, J&M I, no. 471), V, 1 (61r, J&M I, no. 544), etc.

[108] As in V, 2 (61v, J&M I, no. 549), etc.

[109] As in III, 2 (55r, J&M I, no. 491), V, 6 (63r, J&M I, no. 564), etc.

[110] As in III, 3 (11v, J&M I, no. 98) and V, 3 (17r, J&M I, no. 149).

[111] As in IV, 4 (15r, J&M I, no. 133), V, 4 (17v, J&M I, no. 155), etc.

[112] As in III, 2 (11r, J&M I, no. 92), III, 5 (12v, J&M I, no. 111), etc.

[113] In V, 4 (17v, J&M I, no. 155).   [114] In V, 5 (32v, J&M I, no. 293).

[115] As in II, 3 (22v, J&M I, no. 193), III, 5 (25v, J&M I, no. 221), etc.

[116] As in II, 1 (21r, J&M I, no. 180), V, 4, v. 943 (32r, J&M I, no. 287), etc.

[117] In II, 2 (21v, J&M I, no. 186) and V, 7 (33v, J&M I, no. 305).

[118] In II, 1 (80r, J&M I, no. 705) and V, 2 (87v, J&M I, no. 768).

[119] In IV, 5 (86v, J&M I, no. 758).

[120] In IV, 4 (86r, J&M I, no. 753) and V, 4 (88v, J&M I, no. 778).

[121] In I, 1 and 2 (both on 78r, J&M I, nos. 686 and 691).

[122] As in IV, 4 (86r, J&M I, no. 753), V, 6 (89r, J&M I, no. 788), etc.

[123] 65v, J&M I, no. 585.

[124] As in II, 2 (68r, J&M I, no. 604), V, 2 (75r, J&M I, no. 664), etc.

[125] As in III, 5 (71r, J&M I, no. 634), IV, 1 (72r, J&M I, no. 639), etc.

[126] As in III, 4 (70v, J&M I, no. 629), V, 3 (75v, J&M I, no. 669), etc.

[127] Webster, *Monuments Illustrating New Comedy*, p. 210.   [128] *Ibid.*

Dates of garments

Then, apart from the way in which the imagined portrait of Terence is presented, apart from the style of the actors supporting his 'portrait', apart from the hair-styles of both men and women and the beards of the elderly, there is another factor which points to a third-century date for the original of our miniatures. This is the forms of dress of the characters, most particularly the slaves.

So, the long tunic worn by slave girls in the illustrations to *Eunuchus* – whether Pythias, the servant of Thais (pl. IX*a*),[129] or the black girl who has been presented to her[130] – has the shape, the decorative *clavi*, and the wide sleeves embroidered with two bands, which make it exactly like a garment seen in a painting in the Catacomb of Priscilla (pl. IX*b*)[131] which practically every scholar from Wilpert onwards has agreed is third-century. Writing in 1903, Wilpert thought that he could place it in its second half, and sixty-seven years on, Tolotti felt that he could fine-tune it to between the years 280 and 290.[132] More cautiously (and more acceptably) Grabar simply says that it belongs to the mid-third century.[133]

The fact that the attire of the male slaves, like that of the female, is of the third century can be demonstrated by reference to a conclusion which Webster draws from his researches, namely that the wearing by slaves of a long chiton 'with a small mantle like a scarf' is a third-century feature.[134] With the exceptions that we shall come to later, the slaves in our miniatures usually wear the long chiton, and the mantle to which Webster refers is its normal concomitant (see our pls. XII*a* and XIII*b* which illustrate different contexts). The main slave in *Hecyra* is Parmeno, and he never appears without his mantle;[135] when he is joined by two other slaves,[136] they have their mantles, too. Again, the chief slave of

---

129 In V, 1 (30r, J&M I, no. 265) and V, 4 (31v, J&M I, no. 282).

130 In III, 2 (24v, J&M I, no. 204).

131 Wilpert, *Die Malereien der Katakomben Roms*, Tafelband, pl. 8l (in colour).

132 *Ibid.*, Textband, pp. 206–9; and Tolotti, *Il cimitero di Priscilla*, p. 198.

133 Grabar, *The Beginnings of Christian Art*, pl. 117 and p. 320.

134 Webster, *Monuments Illustrating New Comedy*, p. 37.

135 He appears in I, 2 (66v, J&M I, no. 594), III, 1 (69r, J&M I, no. 614), III, 2 (69v, J&M I, no. 619), III, 4 (70v, J&M I, no. 629), V, 3 (75v, J&M I, no. 669) and V, 4 (76r, J&M I, no. 674).

136 In III, 4 (70v, J&M I, no. 629).

Phormio, Geta, has his mantle with him on all but one of his fifteen appearances in the play.[137] Indeed, the mantle is so much part of the 'uniform' of the slaves of our miniatures that the interesting point is not to identify the occasions on which it appears but the rare ones on which it does not, and to try to understand why. The answer to this is usually a sensible and practical one: namely that the slave concerned needs to keep both hands, or at least one of them, free, so that, as with Davus in *Andria*, he can present the small baby to Mysis (IV, 3),[138] or offer up both hands in supplication (IV, 1),[139] like Parmeno in *Eunuchus* (V, 5)[140] or Geta in *Adelphoe* (III, 4);[141] or so that, like another Geta in *Phormio* (V, 6),[142] he can sling his cloak over his shoulder. With Syrus in *Adelphoe* (V, 1),[143] it is different. He is simply drunk.

From this evidence, supplied by Webster, we can say that our miniatures seem to belong to the third century, and we can draw on him still further for an indication that they belong to the earlier part of that century.

As we have already said, the male slaves in our miniatures almost always wear the long chiton. Nonetheless, the short one does make a rare appearance, albeit with some inconsistency. So, the very first illustration of a scene in the manuscript – that to Act I, scene 1 of *Andria*[144] – shows Sosia with two figures (presumably domestic slaves) carrying kitchen equipment. Of these, one wears the long chiton while the other has the short. Elsewhere, we find that even the same slave can wear either form of attire. Davus, in the miniature to Act IV, scene 4 of the play,[145] wears a long chiton, but in the previous scene he has been seen with a short one.[146] On the recto and verso of fol. 32 illustrating Act V, scenes 4 and 5 of *Eunuchus*,[147] Parmeno is depicted in a short chiton, whereas on the adjacent folios on either side he appears in a long one.[148] On rare occasions also, both Syrus and Geta can wear the short chiton as well as

---

[137] He appears in I, 2 (78r, J&M I, no. 691), I, 4 (79v, J&M I, no. 700), II, 1–4 (80r, 81r, 81v and 82v, J&M I, nos. 705, 710, 715 and 720), III, 1–3 (83r–84r, J&M I, nos. 724, 728 and 733), IV, 2–5 (85r–86v, J&M I, nos. 743, 748, 753 and 758) and V, 2 (87v, J&M I, no. 768). For the exception – V, 6 (89r) – see below.

[138] 14v, J&M I, no. 126.   [139] 13r, J&M I, no. 117.

[140] 32v, J&M I, no. 293.   [141] 57r, J&M I, no. 505.

[142] 89r, J&M I, no. 788.   [143] 61r, J&M I, no. 544.   [144] 4v, J&M I, no. 17.

[145] 15r, J&M I, no. 153.   [146] 14v, J&M I, no. 126.

[147] J&M I, nos. 287 and 293.   [148] 31v and 33r, J&M I, nos. 282 and 299.

the long, this in illustrations to *Adelphoe*.[149] (Our pls. XIX*b* and XXVI show them wearing the short.) Now, Webster tells us that this change of style actually took place in the third century,[150] and since he describes some appearances of the long chiton as being 'early third century',[151] we must allow that the vogue was already in being soon after the third century had begun. And since, as we have seen, the artist was aware both of the old fashion and of the new, we may further infer that he was working in a transitional stage, which would be in the early part of the century or at least in its first half.

A *further consideration: the representation of ground-lines*

There is another indication of this in the representation of the ground on which the characters stand. It is often shown more like a shadow than solid earth so that, as Phaedria and Parmeno address each other in the very first scene of *Eunuchus*,[152] they seem to be standing on nothing more substantial than a very faint vestige of ground, and we find the same in other illustrations of the play, such as those to Act IV, scene 3, which features Pythias, Phaedria and Dorias,[153] and Act V, scene 1, which shows Pythias with Thais.[154] This representation of ground is found in other miniatures to the play and in those to other plays, as well. For instance, in those to *Andria*. Here, it can be seen in the pictures for Act I, scene 4,[155] Act II, scenes 1 and 2,[156] Act II, scene 4,[157] Act III, scene 5,[158] Act IV, scenes 1 and 2,[159] Act IV, scene 5[160] and Act V, scenes 3 and 4.[161] As far as the other plays are concerned, we can take as a few random examples the illustrations to Act II, scene 1,[162] Act II, scene 4,[163] and Act III, scene 1[164] of *Heauton timorumenos*, those to the first three scenes of Act III

---

[149] Syrus wears the short chiton in the illustrations to II, 3 (54r, J&M I, no. 476), II, 4 (54v, J&M I, no. 481) and III, 3 (56r, J&M I, no. 501). Geta wears the short chiton in III, 2 (55r, J&M I, no. 491) and III, 3 (56r, J&M I, no. 505).

[150] Webster, *Monuments Illustrating New Comedy*, p. 29.

[151] 'All these are early third century', he says of the examples he is citing (*ibid.*).

[152] 19v, J&M I, no. 168. [153] 27r, J&M I, no. 239.

[154] 30r, J&M I, no. 265. [155] 6v, J&M I, no. 35.

[156] 8r and 8v, J&M I, nos. 50 and 57. [157] 9v, J&M I, no. 64.

[158] 12v, J&M I, no. 111. [159] 13r and 14r, J&M I, nos. 117 and 121.

[160] 15v, J&M I, no. 138. [161] 17r and 17v, J&M I, nos. 149 and 155.

[162] 38r, J&M I, no. 344. [163] 40v, J&M I, no. 362.

[164] 41r, J&M I, no. 369.

of *Adelphoe*,[165] those to the first thirteen scenes of *Hecyra*[166] and those to Act V, scenes 3, 4 and 6 of *Phormio*.[167] The artist does also have other ways of indicating ground, and in large areas of the manuscript gives no indication of it at all: this is true of almost all the miniatures for *Adelphoe* and of the miniatures from Act III, scene 3 of *Heauton timorumenos* to the end of the play (fols. 42v–49v). Nevertheless, it can be said that the primary means of indicating the earth beneath the characters is by the shadow-ground that I have described above. In this, we are reminded of the indication of ground in a vividly sketched painting which helped decorate the vaulting of a villa at Dar Buc Ammera near Zliten (a North African recension of an Alexandrian style),[168] which is not certainly dated but which has been attributed to the end of the second century, or beginning of the third. The representation of a stud farm in a North African mosaic of about the end of the second century from the Maison de Sorothus at Sousse also has the same kind of shadow-ground.[169] In the latter context, it is worth quoting one of the comments made by Dunbabin after her investigations into the mosaics of Roman North Africa. 'It is', she writes, 'an almost universal practice on African mosaics of the second and third centuries to represent ground-lines or shadows beneath the feet of the figures, especially when they form part of a coherent scene.'[170]

Possible provenance of the archetype

There seems, then, enough art-historical evidence to indicate that the models of the Terence pictures were made in the third century AD, and although the various testimonies do not all agree as to the particular decades of that century, we might perhaps be reasonably safe in suggesting the middle ones. This would be given some support by the fact that the comparative material which can be dated most reliably –

---

[165] 55r and 56r, J&M I, nos. 486, 491, 496 and 501.
[166] 65v–72v, J&M I, nos. 585, 589, 594, 599, 604, 609, 614, 619, 624, 629, 634, 639 and 644.
[167] 88r–89r, J&M I, nos. 773, 778 and 788.
[168] See Bianchi Bandinelli, *Rome: the Late Empire*, pl. 241 and p. 434.
[169] Now Sousse, Musée Archéologique, Inv. no. 57.120. Dunbabin, *The Mosaics of Roman North Africa*, pl. XXXI (fig. 81).
[170] *Ibid.*, p. 236.

that of the coiffures – belongs to these years: the hair-style of the Terence 'portrait' is particularly close to the one favoured by emperors between 238 and 249, and that of three of the female masks mirrors one that was in fashion between *c.* 242 and *c.* 267.

There are also slight indications that the models for the Vatican miniatures may derive from North Africa. The similarity in the approach to the representation of ground in the illustrations and in North African mosaics has just been commented on, and the only parallel to the way in which the Terence artist gives a display of masks on shelves is also to be found in North Africa – in the Maison des Masques at Sousse. There were occasions when the original Terence artist simply omitted the mask and presented the character as he was in the flesh, and this happened in his portrayal of one of the young men, Ctesipho, in the illustrations to *Adelphoe*.[171] He appears with his hair shaped in a high dome over the crown and then falling in an S-profile down the nape of the neck, and exactly the same style is worn by the acolyte holding a dish at the top of a Dionysiac scene portrayed in another North African mosaic. This is one in Djemila,[172] which, incidentally, Leschi tentatively dates to 'le début du troisième siècle de notre ère',[173] and which Dunbabin gives to the second or third quarter of the second century.[174] Parallels between the Terence miniatures and the North African mosaics at Sousse will be noted in the next chapter, but perhaps of more consequence is an association of a more direct kind relating to the very unusual garment worn by the bogus eunuch in the play of that name. It has coloured stripes throughout and, to the best of my knowledge, this finds its only parallel in the mosaics later installed in the villa of Piazza Armerina in Sicily, which scholars agree were made by North African artists.[175] On this kind of evidence, there can of course be no certainty, and we need to remember that it is only because of the accidents of history that so many mosaics survive from North

---

[171] See II, 3 (54r, J&M I, no. 476).

[172] Dunbabin, *The Mosaics of Roman North Africa*, pl. LXX (fig. 179).

[173] Leschi, 'Mosaïque à scènes dionysiaques de Djemila-Cuicul', p. 169 and description of pls. VIII and XI.

[174] *The Mosaics of Roman North Africa*, p. 256.

[175] See Wilson, 'Roman Mosaics in Sicily: the African Connection', especially p. 413 and n. 2; and, for a general account of the Piazza Armerina mosaics, Dunbabin, *The Mosaics of Roman North Africa*, pp. 196–212.

Africa to give us a potential for related material. Fortune has been less kind to mosaics in the former European provinces where the ravages of Goths and Vandals and the continuity of urban settlements have all taken their toll.

2

The classical miniatures and the stage

Whatever the exact date or provenance of the models of the Vatican miniatures, no one would doubt that they belong to the late antique period. This being so, we would expect them to give us some insights into the Roman theatre and Roman acting, and, indeed, in 1883 Leo thought that the artist had had some knowledge of the stage.[1] However, others – particularly Jachmann, whose views will be examined in detail at the end of the next chapter[2] and who was writing in 1924 – were to take a contrary position. Despite one or two dissenting voices, this position has found scholarly acceptance since. It was particularly endorsed by Jones and Morey, who gave general currency to it. In 1931, they wrote that 'the dependence of the miniatures on actual stage-representation of the plays, has been repeatedly considered and rejected by ... writers on our subject ... they are essentially literary creations';[3] and, again, that the miniatures 'are the product of literary rather than theatrical usage'.[4] These ideas have held the field over the past six decades. Nonetheless, there are very clear indications that the original artist *did* have an awareness of theatrical practices and traditions.

GESTURES CLEARLY KNOWN TO THE STAGE

One of his gestures, for example, could have had no possible application except on the stage. It occurs in the miniature associated with Act IV, scene 2 of *Hecyra*[5] where Sostrata is seen telling her son that, for his sake,

---

[1] Leo, 'Die Ueberlieferungsgeschichte der terenzischen Komödien', pp. 337–8 and 341.
[2] See below, pp. 96–100.   [3] J&M II, 203–4.   [4] *Ibid.*, p. 204.
[5] 72v, J&M I, no. 644.

she has decided to go into the country. On the other side of the stage, the illustrator has shown her husband, Laches, holding up a half-closed fist from which his little finger points upwards (pl. X*a*), and the meaning of this gesture is revealed by his first words in the next scene: 'Quem cum istoc sermonem habueris procul hinc stans accepi, uxor.'[6] In other words, as others have observed, this is the gesture for eavesdropping. And very useful it must have been on the Roman stage, which was virtually an empty platform with very few accessories so that the actors could clearly see each other. Yet, by this simple device, one of them could alert the spectators to the fact that he was meant to be out of sight of the others. In Act IV, scene 3 of *Phormio*,[7] Antipho tells the audience that he is waiting for the slave Geta, but on the approach of his father and uncle, he remarks that he is fearful of what advice the latter may give to his father (vv. 607–8) and decides to draw back and listen to what they have to say about his future without their seeing him. Although he makes asides to the audience, it is only in the next scene that he reveals himself and, in the meantime, he has been eavesdropping as he reveals by this signal for it (pl. XXIX*a*). Now it is obvious enough that no eavesdropper would really draw conspicuous attention to himself in this way. Clearly it was a convention of the Roman theatre, and very well known it must have been, for it is used in one play as a visual quip which could only have made its point to an audience thoroughly familiar with it. The play is *Heauton timorumenos*, and we are at a point in the action (IV, 4)[8] where Dromo is being told that, if he has any sense, he will assume ignorance about what has just happened. He briefly replies with the comment 'mutum dices'[9] and at the same time makes this gesture. It is not without wit since the eavesdropper by definition is a mute observer.

The association of this signal with silence may explain its appearance in an illustration of *Hecyra*. The action of the play opens with the courtesan Philotis criticizing the ways of men towards women of her class and at the same time she makes this gesture (pl. X*b*).[10] Now this can have nothing to do with eavesdropping since there is only one other person on stage – the person she is addressing – and it may well have been intended

[6] *Hecyra* 607: 'I have been standing within earshot, wife, and have heard your conversation.'

[7] 85v, J&M I, no. 748. [8] 45r, J&M I, no. 502.

[9] *Heauton timorumenos* 748: 'Reckon me as dumb.' [10] 66r, J&M I, no. 589.

for the spectators. The Prologue, who has only just left the stage, has been telling them that two earlier productions of the play were disrupted by the interruptions of other forms of entertainment and by the shouting and screaming of their supporters, and he begs that this, the third production, be given a quiet and proper hearing. In fact, almost his last words are a plea for the audience to give their silence – 'date silentium' (v. 55). We might, then, interpret this gesture, given at the very opening of the action of the play by the first person to speak in it, as a visual reinforcement of what the Prologue has said.

As an indicator of eavesdropping, this gesture must have been unique to the stage. But there are two others in our Terence which were certainly known to it even though they were also in use elsewhere. One was the gesture for profound thought, which appears in contexts clearly associated with the theatre as we shall see later.[11] The second is known to us from Quintilian.

In his famous work on the education of the orator written at the end of the first century AD, the *Institutio oratoria*, Quintilian described one of his rhetorical gestures as follows: 'est et illa caua et rara et supra umeri altitudinem elata cum quodam motu uelut hortatrix manus.'[12] The importance of his account from our point of view is in its continuation, which says that 'a peregrinis scholis tamen prope recepta, tremula, scaenica':[13] in other words, actors were familiar with this particular gesture but chose to embellish it a little and make it more like a wave of the hand. We see examples of it in our miniatures (pl. XVI*a* and *b*), as we shall demonstrate in our next chapter,[14] and as a stage gesture it is also represented in a painting from the Casa dei Dioscuri in Naples of a nursing woman addressing another person.[15] If we add this gesture to

[11] See below, pp. 31–2 and 85–6.

[12] XI.iii.103 (ed. Radermacher II, 347): 'there is also that gesture in which the hand is hollowed, with the fingers spread, and raised above the shoulder with a motion suggestive of exhortation.' In oratorical terms, this gesture is seen in use in a first-century BC bronze statue, said to be of Aulus Metullus, which was dredged up in six parts from Lake Trasimeno. See Strong, *The Classical World*, fig. 98.

[13] 'The tremulous motion almost generally adopted by foreign schools is fit only for the stage.'

[14] See below, pp. 40–4.

[15] Bieber, *The History of the Greek and Roman Theater*, fig. 773.

those for eavesdropping and thought, then we can say that three of the Terence gestures were known to the Roman stage.

QUINTILIAN AND THE TERENCE MINIATURES

Since we have mentioned Quintilian in connection with one gesture in our Terence and shall have cause to do so for others, it is worth noting here that this is not the first time that scholars have associated his writings with our pictures. Leo did so already in 1883,[16] and Weston in 1903.[17] However, the objectives of both were very different from our own since they believed that, by demonstrating parallels between gestures described by the Roman orator and those appearing in the Terence, they could show that the original illustrations predated Quintilian himself and belonged, Weston believed, to the period 'of Roscius and the theatre of his day and perhaps, by tradition, the theatre of Ambivius Turpio [the supporter and producer of Terence] as well'.[18] Weston's exposition was the more extensive and, if we look at it, we shall see how unsuccessful his particular arguments were. For one thing, he confined his attention simply to the illustrations of *Phormio*, and for another, he seems to have believed that the Vatican, Paris and Milan versions (the latter two will be discussed in the next chapter) all had the same authority and that they shared this with a mid-twelfth-century English copy at Oxford,[19] which – however admirable the Romanesque style of its miniatures – has little claim to any independent legitimacy. More significant than this, however, is the following. Of the eight relationships Weston claimed to have found, only one is correct; another might be said to be dubious but the rest are certainly inaccurate.[20] Since Weston, efforts to see a relationship

---

[16] 'Die Ueberlieferungsgeschichte der terenzischen Komödien', pp. 337–41.

[17] Weston, 'The Illustrated Terence Manuscripts'.   [18] *Ibid.*, p. 54.

[19] Oxford, Bodleian Library, Auct. F. 2. 13. See J&M II, 68–93.

[20] Weston, 'The Illustrated Terence Manuscripts', pp. 50–3. The correct one is his reference to Quintilian XI.iii.92. The dubious one, which I personally find unacceptable, is to XI.iii.123. In my detailing of the rest, Q will stand for Quintilian and my references to the play will be, like Weston's, to *Phormio*.

Weston relates Q XI.iii.95 to Geta and Demipho in IV, 3, but the gesture given by both is quite different and will be discussed in the pages that follow. The gesture of Q XI.iii.96 cannot be read into those given by Geta and Antipho in III, 3: Geta's hand is near his chin not his chest, and Antipho's is not being flung down. Q's gesture for approval (XI.iii.101) is different from that ascribed to Geta in II, 3. It is similar to the

between Quintilian and the Terence have been dropped, and in 1931 Jones and Morey attempted a complete rebuttal of the view that such a relationship existed.[21] The time, nevertheless, would seem ripe for a fresh, and more balanced, appraisal and this we shall endeavour to give in our later pages.

With reference to Quintilian, it is also worth noting that he refers in his *Institutio* to the variety of masks used by the actors of his day, and draws special attention to one of them. It was not the normal mask, which usually simply expressed sex, age and appearance, but a double one which portrayed two very different moods, enabling the actor to play the role of someone either in a bad temper or in a good. Quintilian explained that the variation was obtained by a difference in the positioning of the eyebrows of the mask. One eyebrow was raised and the other lowered, so that the actor wishing to present himself at one time in a passion and at another calm would display the side of the mask that was most appropriate: 'in comoediis uero ... pater ille, cuius praecipuae partes sunt, quia interim concitatus, interim lenis est, altero erecto, altero composito est supercilio, atque id ostendere maxime latus actoribus moris est, quod cum iis, quas agunt, partibus congruat.'[22] All this is well known, as also the fact – already pointed out by Robert[23] – that the same mask is described in much the same terms by Pollux, the Greek rhetorician of the second century AD, who includes it in his list of masks used in New Comedy. Now it is significant to our argument that just such a mask is represented in the Terence pictures (pl. XI) as, indeed, Robert also pointed out many years ago. We have seen earlier that five of the six plays

one given to Chremes in IV, 3 but not, in fact, the same as we shall see from a consideration of it later. The gesture described in Q XI.iii.103 is unlike the one claimed for Dorio in III, 2 and Cratinus and Crito in II, 4. Demipho's gesture in V, 2 is quite dissimilar to that given in Q XI.iii.104. Q XI.iii.124 speaks of touching the breast with the finger-tips of the hollowed hand. Weston claims that a 'modification' of this gesture 'occurs several times', namely with Antipho in I, 3 and III, 1, Phaedria in III, 3 and Nausistrata in V, 9; the 'modification', however, is a different gesture, in which the character points a finger towards the face.

[21] J&M II, 206–9.

[22] XI.iii.74 (ed. Radermacher II, 341): 'in stage-plays ... the father who has a main part, because he is sometimes enraged and sometimes calm, has [a mask with] one eyebrow raised and the other down; and it is the custom among actors to display the most that side that accords with the action as they perform it.'

[23] *Die Masken der neueren attischen Komoedie*, p. 29.

are prefaced with a display, on shelves, of the masks that will be required in the play, and this one occurs in the array before the very first play, *Andria*. It is second from the right on the first shelf from the bottom,[24] and its right eyebrow is very decidedly up and its left one very decidedly down. The same mask is also drawn in a related copy of the late antique original, which was the one that Robert was using and which we ourselves shall come to later.[25]

Obviously, this double mask could have served no purpose except on the stage, but the more usual ones in our miniatures belong to the theatre also. Webster, the distinguished authority on the subject, is our source for this. He speaks of the Terence masks preserving the traditions of the Hellenic originals 'most faithfully'.[26] In fact, in his catalogue of monuments of New Comedy, he treats them as genuine artifacts in their own right.[27] In one place he is even more specific and compares a marble mask of a eunuch (it is inscribed 'EUNUCHU') in the theatre of Khamissa, which he dates around 200 AD, to that worn by Chaerea in his impersonation of a eunuch in Terence's play of that name.[28] We might add that another expert on the classical theatre, Bieber, has given her opinion that the stage properties are authentic to the Roman stage: 'I cannot', she says of our miniatures, 'see how a purely literary creation based on reading could give to all characters, in most cases, the right theatrical masks, garments and outfits.'[29]

The very means of characterizing the classes in our pictures are part and parcel of what we know of the Roman theatre, and to demonstrate this we can again draw on Quintilian. He was not anxious to associate his own professional art of oratory with the plebeian craft of acting, but as we have already seen, he did, in his *Institutio*, make occasional comments on the theatre of his day. One of them concerned the stage convention by which the more elevated members of society were distinguished by their decorum, and the more servile ones by their unseemly ebullience: 'in

---

[24] 3r, J&M I, no. 7.

[25] BN lat. 7899 (about which more will be said in the next chapter), 2v, J&M I, no. 6.

[26] *Monuments Illustrating New Comedy*, p. 210.   [27] *Ibid.*, pp. 30–2 and 210–11.

[28] *Ibid.*, pp. 311 and ix.

[29] *A History of the Greek and Roman Theater*, p. 297, n. 26. Duckworth, *The Nature of Roman Comedy*, p. 88, disagrees and says that the characters do not all have the correct garments. He gives no particular instances, but an occasional slip on the part of an artist giving the right attire to 381 drawings of actors seems to me to be acceptable.

fabulis iuuenum, senum, militum, matronarum grauior ingressus est, serui, ancillulae, parasiti, piscatores citatius mouentur.'[30] Now we see just this in our pictures where the more important characters stand and move with decorum while unworthy persons are shown at times in an over-energetic state, twisting their bodies unnecessarily about, and pulling and tugging at their mantles, as we especially see in the figure of Davus in an illustration to *Andria* IV, 5.[31] The contrast is exemplified in the illustration to Act V, scene 5 of the same play[32] where the sedate posture of Pamphilus and Charinus is in complete contrast with the bending and contorting figure of the slave Davus (pl. XII*a*). In fact, a similar contrast is made in the portrayal of a scene from comedy in a late second- or early third-century mosaic at Sousse in Tunisia,[33] where the posture of the slave (pl. XII*b*) is sufficiently close to that of the bent, but still energetic, figure of Davus to suggest that both artists were conscious of the same tradition.

One aspect of this over-activity of the slave was to show him at times in a great hurry, and it is an accepted fact that this idea of the running slave, the 'seruus currens', was an entrenched theme in classical comedy. Indeed, Terence refers to it himself. In his Prologue to *Eunuchus*, he says that, if others argue that he should not make use of the types of earlier playwrights, then he will not be able to bring on a running slave ('currentem seruom') and other stock characters.[34] There are further references to the running slave in the Prologue to *Heauton timorumenos*. The play was first produced in 153 BC, when the Prologue was delivered by Lucius Ambivius Turpio who both referred to the presence of a running slave in a recent play, and included the running slave first in a list of characters frequently portrayed in comedy.[35] Statuettes of the characters of classical comedy survive to reflect the types of the Greek and Roman theatre and many of them are of stock theatrical slaves. These include running slaves – for example, three of the second century BC deriving from Myrina and Smyrna[36] – and we also have an engraved gem

---

[30] XI.iii.112 (ed. Radermacher II, 349): 'On the stage the gait of young men, of old men, of military characters and of matrons is somewhat slow; while male or female slaves, parasites and fishermen move with greater agility.'

[31] 15v, J&M I, no. 138.   [32] 18r, J&M I, no. 161.

[33] Salomonson, *Mosaïques romaines de Tunisie*, p. 25 (no. 9) and pls. 10–11.

[34] *Eunuchus* 36.   [35] *Heauton timorumenos* 31 and 37.

[36] Webster, *Monuments Illustrating New Comedy*, MT 30 (p. 83), MT 31 (p. 84) and ZT 29 (p. 93).

with a depiction of a hastening servant.[37] In the Terence pictures, this traditional feature appears on a number of occasions. So, Davus hurries, rushes or skips in the illustrations of *Andria* (II, 2 and 6, IV, 1 and 3, and V, 5),[38] and we see the same nimbleness in the movements of Parmeno in the miniatures to *Eunuchus* (III, 2 and V, 5),[39] in those of Syrus in *Adelphoe* (II, 3 and III, 3)[40] and of Geta in the same play,[41] in those of another Parmeno in *Hecyra*,[42] and in those of another Geta in two scenes of *Phormio*.[43] On the first of the latter two occasions (I, 2), this Geta is met almost head-on by another rushing slave so that an imminent collision seems very probable. The illustrations to five of the six plays of Terence have their running slave, or slaves.

Slaves are the butt of mockery in our pictures not only for their over-ebullience but also for another supposed characteristic. This is the vulgarity of their body language, and since it is in terms known to Quintilian, it could hardly have been newly invented by the artist. One example of this is the posture of standing or moving with one's legs wide apart, which Quintilian had stigmatized as being unbecoming at the best, and indecent at the worst: 'uaricare supra modum et in stando deforme est et accedente motu prope obscenum.'[44] In our miniatures, this posture is adopted by the slave Parmeno in an illustration to *Eunuchus*,[45] and by a slave of Simo's in the first scene of Act I of *Andria*.[46] Here, a contrast is made between the dignity of the master and the gaucheness of the servant. Another posture which attracted Quintilian's disdain was accompanying the speech with movements of the elbow, placing the arm across the body instead of extending it as in a more respectable gesture of address: 'adhuc peius aliqui transuersum brachium proferunt et cubito

---

[37] *Ibid.*, UJ 18 (p. 93).

[38] 8v, J&M I, no. 57; 10r, J&M I, no. 78; 13r, J&M I, no. 117; 14v, J&M I, no. 126; and 18r, J&M I, no. 161.

[39] 24v, J&M I, no. 204; and 32v, J&M I, no. 293.

[40] 54r, J&M I, no. 476; and 56r, J&M I, no. 501.   [41] III, 4 (57r, J&M I, no. 505).

[42] III, 1 (69r, J&M I, no. 614).

[43] In I, 2 (78r, J&M I, no. 691) and IV, 4 (86r, J&M I, no. 793).

[44] XI.iii.125 (ed. Radermacher II, 352): 'to place the legs wide apart is unbecoming if one stands still, and almost obscene if one moves in that posture.' Similarly, 'prolato dextro stare ... deforme est' (XI.iii.124; ed. Radermacher II, 352): 'to stand with the right leg advanced ... is unbecoming.'

[45] V, 4, v. 943 (32r, J&M I, no. 287).   [46] 4v, J&M I, no. 17.

pronuntiant.'[47] This also is seen in our pictures. The posture is taken up by Davus in both Act I, scene 2 and Act III, scene 5 of *Andria*.[48] The pushing out of the stomach attracted further reprobation from the orator as being impolite and unmannerly: 'pectus ac uenter ne proiciantur, obseruandum: pandant enim posteriora et est odiosa omnis supinitas.'[49] This is exactly what the slaves Geta and Davus do in the illustrations to *Adelphoe* V, 6 and *Andria* IV, 4 respectively.[50] Geta here also shrugs his shoulders, an action, according to the *Institutio*, which was mean and servile as well as being suggestive of dishonesty: 'umerorum raro decens adleuatio atque contractio est ... gestum quendam humilem atque seruilem et quasi fraudulentum facit.'[51] Parmeno, who does the same in *Eunuchus* (V, 4),[52] becomes the very epitome of boorishness as he also stands with his legs apart and his body slumped as if out of control. Now all this might indicate no more than that the artist wished to continue the lampooning of the slave population, but there is one hint that here, also, he may have been drawing on earlier traditions. This is the fact that, if his slaves stand with their feet apart to proclaim their coarseness, so also does a terracotta representation of a comic slave dating from the second century BC,[53] and also another slave in a painting of a stage performance from Pompeii[54] considered to belong to the first century AD. The fact that this particular indication of boorishness has been transmitted over three centuries would certainly suggest that it was part of an ongoing tradition.

Slaves in the Terence are pilloried not only for their uncouthness but also for their pretentiousness. This too is in keeping with a theatrical tradition, as we know from Plautus. In the *Miles gloriosus*, which he wrote about 206 BC, Plautus records the amusement of an old gentleman,

---

[47] XI.iii.93 (ed. Radermacher II, 345): 'what is still worse, some bring their arm across [their chest] and speak over their elbow.'

[48] 6r, J&M I, no. 25; and 12v, J&M I, no. 111.

[49] XI.iii.122 (ed. Radermacher II, 351): 'care should be taken that the chest and stomach be not thrust forward, for this may open up the posterior parts to view, and all bending backwards is distasteful.'

[50] 63r, J&M I, no. 564; and 15r, J&M I, no. 133.

[51] XI.iii.83 (ed. Radermacher II, 343): 'the shrugging of the shoulders is seldom fitting ... for it begets a gesture that is lowly and servile and as it were knavish.'

[52] 32r, J&M I, no. 287.

[53] Webster, *Monuments Illustrating New Comedy*, UT 53 (p. 150).

[54] Bieber, *The History of the Greek and Roman Theater*, fig. 395.

Periplectomenus, at the antics of the slave Palaestrio in trying to advertise to the world that he is deep in thought by various actions: by tapping his chest, smacking his thigh, shaking his head, and so on. Included in the charade of meditation presented by the slave was a gesture which Plautus later particularly fastens on; it is where the slave uses his arm as a pillar for his chin:

> illuc sis uide,
> quem ad modum astitit, seuero fronte curans, cogitans ...
> ecce autem aedificat: columnam mento suffigit suo.[55]

This resting of the chin on the fist, or hand, had of course been used by artists as an indicator of pondering over the centuries. However, they had usually associated it with divine thinkers, like the well-known figure in the Portland vase which has been said by Haynes to represent a sea-god if not Poseidon himself,[56] or the sculpted figure of Polyhymnia in a Rhodian sculpture now in Basel,[57] or personifications like that of Asia or Persia represented in a Boscoreale figure-cycle,[58] or those of high estate, as Medea musing on the murder of her children in a mural from Pompeii,[59] or philosophers like the pensive figure in a mosaic said to represent the Academy of Plato from Torre Annunziata.[60] As we shall see later, it was allowed in the Terence illustrations to two of the graver characters, but the idea of it being adopted by a slave – one of the lowest class aping the ways of the highest – was clearly a subject of derision. It no doubt appealed to the same elementary sense of humour that led the cartoonists of magazines like *Punch* in the days before the First World War to poke fun at the housemaid for putting on the airs and graces of

---

[55] *Miles gloriosus* 200–1 and 209: 'Just look at him, how he stands with wrinkled brow, worrying and thinking! ... Look! Now he's building, setting a column under his chin!'

[56] Haynes, *The Portland Vase*, p. 17 and pl. V.

[57] Charbonneaux, Martin and Villard, *Hellenistic Art*, pl. 310.

[58] *Ibid.*, pl. 134. For this cycle see Andreae, 'Rekonstruktion des grossen Oecus'. On the interpretation, see Fittschen, 'Zum Figurenfries der Villa von Boscoreale', pp. 95–6. Fittschen's view is that it is a personification of Asia who is sitting at the feet of Macedonia, but he notes that Robertson had suggested Persia rather than Asia.

[59] Charbonneaux, Martin and Villard, *Hellenistic Art*, pl. 118; and Ling, *Roman Painting*, pl. 146. It is dated to the second quarter of the first century AD.

[60] Anthony, *A History of Mosaics*, pl. 1. The subject of this 'philosopher mosaic' in Naples has been variously interpreted. See most recently Gaiser, *Das Philosophenmosaik in Neapel*.

her social superiors. Like the latter, it was presumably a stock joke, good for an easy laugh, and to take but one or two examples, the survival of a bronze statuette of a pondering slave from the late Hellenistic or early Roman period (pl. XIII*a*),[61] and of terracotta figurines of the subject from the first century BC,[62] will indicate that the pondering slave belonged to a long history of stage representations in art as well as on the boards. Parmeno parodies this gesture of quiet contemplation in our miniatures by also walking in one direction and turning his head in another while still clutching his mantle (pl. XIII*b*),[63] and in *Andria* the slave Davus hardly projects an image of relaxed meditation as he slouches on crossed feet.[64] Another slave using the gesture is Geta in Act III, scene 3 of *Phormio*.[65]

As it happens, Plautus can give us yet further evidence for the traditionalism of our pictures. Duckworth draws our attention to a remark he gives to Ergasilus in his play *Captiui*:[66]

> eodem pacto ut comici serui solent,
> coniciam in collum pallium.[67]

According to Duckworth, the habit of casting the cloak over the shoulder to which Ergasilus' comment attests would have been intended to enable the slaves to bustle about more energetically. Our own interest is to see how actors on the stage had seized on this very characteristic from the early Hellenistic period, as we know from a statuette which survives from about then.[68] When, therefore, our Terence artist portrays the slave Geta doing just this in his illustration to Act V, scene 6 of *Phormio*,[69] we can say that this offers yet further grounds for supposing that he was following a well-known tradition.

And, while noting the relationship between these figurees and our

---

[61] Vienna, Kunsthistorisches Museum, Inv. no. VI 281; see Webster, *Monuments Illustrating New Comedy*, EB 2 (p. 97).

[62] See *ibid.*, ZT 26 (p. 93) and UT 42 (p. 148).

[63] *Eunuchus* II, 2 (21v, J&M I, no. 186).   [64] IV, 2 (14r, J&M I, no. 121).

[65] 84r, J&M I, no. 733.   [66] *The Nature of Roman Comedy*, p. 91.

[67] *Captiui* 778–9: 'I will throw my cloak over my shoulder just as slaves in comedies usually do.'

[68] Webster, *Monuments Illustrating New Comedy*, MT 26 (p. 83). Other slaves with cloaks over the shoulder but seated are seen in UT 72 (p. 152), UT 95 (p. 155) and UT 96 (p. 155).

[69] 89r, J&M I, no. 788.

miniatures, it is worthwhile to call attention to a gesture that has nothing specifically to do with the slave population, but with the indication of sadness by all classes. There were a number of ways of showing this emotion in the classical world, including tearing the hair or breast, striking the head, clawing at the cheek,[70] beginning to cry and covering up the face with one or both hands or attempting to cover the visage with a garment,[71] laying the cheek against the open hand,[72] lowering the head to gaze at the floor with the hand to the chin,[73] and placing one hand over the head while the other is positioned above it as if to strike.[74] Among all these possibilities, the gesture that the Terence artist chose to indicate sadness was one that had been in use in Old Comedy. This consisted of placing a disconsolate hand either near or against the cheek, and it is instructive to see how closely this gesture in a surviving figurine of the period, now in Athens,[75] parallels the one selected by our own illustrator (pl. XIV*a* and *b*). The only explanation is that this particular gesture was traditional to the stage and, in our next chapter, we shall see other examples of its use in the Vatican manuscript.

There is a good deal of evidence, then, to show that our illustrator had a close knowledge of the classical stage and its traditions. His gesture for eavesdropping could only have been used on the classical stage, and we have seen that three others of his gestures were known to it. His double mask was a particular feature of the theatre, and both his characterization of the classes and the ways in which he parodies the slaves reflect earlier stage-traditions. On the authority of such distinguished specialists as Webster and Bieber, we may add that his masks and stage properties are authentic. In the next chapter, we shall endeavour to show that so also are his dramatic gestures.

---

[70] Sittl, *Die Gebärden der Griechen und Römer*, pp. 66, 71 and 274; Neumann, *Gesten und Gebärden in der griechischen Kunst*, pp. 86 and 89.

[71] Sittl, *Die Gebärden der Griechen und Römer*, p. 275.

[72] Neumann, *Gesten und Gebärden in der griechischen Kunst*, p. 149.   [73] *Ibid.*, p. 136.

[74] *Ibid.*, p. 87.

[75] Webster, *Monuments Illustrating Old and Middle Comedy*, AT 73*a* (p. 88).

3

Dramatic gestures in the miniatures

The double mask described by Quintilian was unique. As we have seen, the normal mask was so inflexible that actors would have depended very largely on gestures to express their feelings, and there are a number of these in our illustrations of Terence. This naturally raises the question of whether they are authentic to the theatre or merely literary compilations dreamed up by a later artist to adorn the pages: visual confections, as it were, which have no more relationship to the realities of the Roman stage than nineteenth-century illustrations of Shakespeare have to the Elizabethan theatre. The question is an important one, for if the Terence gestures are genuine and their meanings can be recovered, they should give us a new insight into Roman acting.

Following the traditional judgement that our pictures are unrelated to Roman acting, the conventional view for some decades now has been that the gestures, too, have no association with the classical theatre, and J.-C. Schmitt was content to repeat a time-worn concept when he remarked in his recent survey of medieval gestures that there was no evidence that those in the Terence go back to 'des modèles anciens inspirés de représentations théâtrales véritables'.[1] Yet, as we have seen, four of them – those for eavesdropping, pondering, grief, and the one described by Quintilian – were certainly in use in the Roman theatre, and the first was confined to it. Despite all this, the supposed lack of a relationship in the past has led to a lack of scholarly interest in the gestures, so that historians of art and of the theatre alike have tended to ignore them. The primary purpose of this chapter is to examine them in detail.

One or two of them are obvious enough and call for no explanation.

[1] Schmitt, *La Raison des gestes*, p. 98.

Such is the pointing gesture used by Sostrata, for example, in the illustration to Act III, scene 2 of *Adelphoe*[2] when she points to Geta as she comments to her old nurse on his strange behaviour (v. 305), and by Syrus, later on in the same play, when he points to his lip to support his claim that it has been split by his young master (IV, 2, v. 559).[3] Another straightforward gesture is the *adlocutio* one for speech, in which the speaker crooks one or two fingers (here usually two) towards the person or persons addressed as if to hold his, or their, attention.[4] This gesture was a commonplace of classical and medieval art, and seems to have survived into the twentieth century in Austrian schools.[5] However, there are a good many more which are less straightforward, and for help with one or two of these we can look again to Quintilian. His occasional asides about the contemporary theatre have already been of assistance to us, but even where his text is more centrally focused on his counsels to the budding orator about the use of gestures, he contributes observations relevant to our study. The significance of those observations can be overplayed, as has been noted in the previous chapter, but they nonetheless provide some useful evidence.

QUINTILIAN'S GESTURES

Certainly three of the gestures he describes for the orator can be found in our illustrations where they carry the rhetorician's meanings.

The first is the one for exhortation mentioned in the last chapter, on which we shall expand shortly. The second is one in which all the fingers are bent except the middle one which is curved to meet the thumb. According to Quintilian, this is useful when reproaching or refuting: 'gestus ille ... quo medius digitus in pollicem contrahitur explicitis tribus ... in exprobrando et coarguendo acer atque instans.'[6] We find the

---

[2] BN lat. 7899 (hereafter P), 105r; Vatican, Vat. lat. 3868 (hereafter C), 55r; J&M I, nos. 490–1.

[3] P 111v (where Syrus is pointing too high), C 58r, J&M I, nos. 514–15.

[4] On 67v of C (J&M I, no. 599), where Laches and his wife address each other, Laches uses both fingers in the gesture and his wife one.

[5] Gombrich, 'Ritualized Gesture and Expression in Art', p. 394.

[6] XI.iii.92 (ed. Radermacher II, 345): 'that gesture ... in which the middle finger is drawn to the thumb, with the other three fingers open ... is crisp and urgent when reproaching and refuting.'

gesture used in exactly the latter sense by Hegio in *Phormio* (II, 4)[7] when he is refuting the legal opinion given by Cratinus on the question of Antipho's marriage (pl. XV*a*). Cratinus has claimed that it is null and void but Hegio is saying that, on the contrary, it has been legally entered into, and must therefore stand (vv. 454–5). The third gesture is an imperative. It consists of directing the extended index finger towards the ground and it indicates insistence: 'is ... uersus in terram et quasi pronus urget.'[8] In the Terence, this same gesture looks commanding enough and it conforms to the appropriate context, for it is used by Chremes in *Heauton timorumenos* (III, 2)[9] when he is laying down the law on how the difficulties of Clinia could have been resolved, before giving peremptory instructions to a slave to attend to the business in hand (pl. XV*b*). As it happens, this particular gesture was also described and illustrated by a remarkable English writer of the mid-seventeenth century, a physician named John Bulwer, who, taking over a phrase from Bacon[10] that Bacon himself had borrowed from King James I,[11] wrote that 'as the Tongue speaketh to the Eare, so Gesture speaketh to the Eye'.[12] Since, in Bulwer's view, gesture was the natural and universal language of mankind, he decided to scour all sources, including the bible with its Hebrew version, classical and patristic writings, works of art, coins, etc., in order to formulate a kind of universal encyclopaedia of gesture, which he also had illustrated. His account of this gesture is as follows: 'The *Index* (the rest compos'd into a *Fist*) turn'd down perpendicular; doth *urge*, *inculcate* and drive the point into the heads of the Auditours.'[13]

These three gestures are authenticated by the Roman authority on

---

[7] P 159v (where the gesture is very unclear), C 82v, J&M I, nos. 719–20.

[8] XI.iii.94 (ed. Radermacher II, 345–6): 'when directed down towards the ground, this finger insists.'

[9] P 80r, C 42r, J&M I, nos. 374–5.

[10] *The twoo Bookes of Francis Bacon. Of the Proficience and Aduancement of Learning, Diuine and Humane* (London, 1605), Book II, 37r: 'As the Tongue speaketh to the Eare, so the gesture speaketh to the Eye.'

[11] King James I, *Basilicon Doron* (Edinburgh, 1599; facsimile edition, Scolar Press, Menston, 1969), p. 135: 'as the tongue speaketh to the eares, so doth the gesture speake to the eies of the auditoure.'

[12] Bulwer, *Chirologia*, sig. A5rv (prefatory epistle 'To the Candid and Ingenious Reader', second and third pages).

[13] Bulwer, *Chironomia*, p. 79. The *Chironomia* is bound with the *Chirologia* and separately paginated.

oratory and conform to his descriptions. Yet this still leaves us with the vast majority of others for which he gives us no help, and to understand these we shall need to turn from external witness to internal analysis. But, before embarking on this, we shall need to remind ourselves that, as well as the illustrated Terence in the Vatican, which textual critics have given the siglum 'C' and on which we have so far concentrated our attention, three others have survived from the Carolingian period.

CAROLINGIAN ILLUSTRATED MANUSCRIPTS OF TERENCE

The most important, by far, is now Paris, Bibliothèque Nationale de France, lat. 7899, and is usually designated 'P'. It was made in the second or third quarter of the ninth century.[14] Jones and Morey say that any examination of it will reveal that its most conspicuous feature is its close adherence to the Vatican pictures whereby the observer 'will be convinced without further demonstration of the derivation of both sets of miniatures from the same archetype',[15] a viewpoint which they reiterate elsewhere, as when they comment that 'the two series are derived from the same model'.[16] This, however, is challenged by Grant who, after an extended analysis, argues for a relationship that is less that of sisters, as Jones and Morey propose, than that of cousins, or second cousins.[17] Nevertheless, no one would doubt that the two manuscripts belong to the same family.

The Paris manuscript was in the library of Saint-Denis in the thirteenth century as we know from a library mark in it and also from an inscription on fol. 41r: 'Iste liber est de sancto dionisuo [*sic*] en francia.' However, on the basis of its artistic style and script, Jones and Morey have assigned it to Reims,[18] a view agreed by Bischoff[19] and generally accepted by scholars. Its illustrations (by two artists) adhere carefully to those of the archetypal miniatures in terms of compositions, although they depart from them in terms of style and replace the late antique one of the original Roman model with the sketchy impressionistic style that

---

[14] Jones and Morey (II, 67) believed that P was made 'not long after 820 (the approximate date of C)'. More recent scholarship has favoured a date in the third quarter of the ninth century: see, for example, Villa, *La 'Lectura Terentii'*, p. 394 (no. 440).

[15] J&M II, 56.   [16] *Ibid.*, p. 66.

[17] Grant, *Studies in the Textual Tradition of Terence*, ch. 5, pp. 136–54. He gives his own stemma on p. 154 which refines an earlier one of Webb's.

[18] J&M II, 63–6.   [19] In a personal letter of 8 April 1978.

was then in vogue in the Reims area. Nevertheless, for our present purpose, it is their recording of the original gestures that matters. Indeed, in this they are second in importance only to the Vatican copies which they can correct or clarify at times. We shall therefore draw on both manuscripts, using each to balance the other, and shall indicate any discrepancies between them in the footnotes. And it would be strange if there were none. It is an axiom of textual criticism that the transmission of texts before the days of printing often led to scribal errors on the part of the copyists, and it would be remarkable if, in the transmission of 381 figures in the cycle of our pictures, there were no mistake on the part of the artists. We might add that the drawings in the Paris manuscript often give a clearer rendering of the gestures than we find in the Vatican manuscript, and both in this and in their technique, they can be more closely aligned with drawings of the Anglo-Saxon period to which we shall wish to relate them later.

There is a second Carolingian copy in the French Bibliothèque Nationale, lat. 7900, designated 'J',[20] and this was probably made in the second half of the ninth century at Corbie although an inscription on its first folio shows that that leaf (and possibly the whole manuscript) was at Fleury in the twelfth century; the leaf is, however, an addition, and may perhaps not have been bound with the rest until the sixteenth century.[21] It is generally agreed that the pictures of this copy are closely associated with those of the two manuscripts already described. Nevertheless, they will make no contribution to our enquiry since they are careless as well as being incomplete.

Another Carolingian manuscript with illustrations of Terence survives in the Biblioteca Ambrosiana at Milan (S.P. 4 bis; formerly H 75 inf.).[22] It used to be accredited to the vicinity of Orléans, but Bischoff gives it to the neighbourhood of Reims,[23] and it can be dated to the end of the ninth or beginning of the tenth century. It is designated 'F'. Its first thirty miniatures have been lost, but those that remain are attractively drawn and should be of value in our attempts to recover the classical originals if all the claims of Jones and Morey are correct. They say that

[20] See J&M II, 94–101.

[21] Bischoff, 'Hadoardus and the Manuscripts of Classical Authors from Corbie', p. 53.

[22] See J&M II, 102–19.

[23] See Reynolds, *Texts and Transmission*, p. 417, n. 42. He also gave the same information to me.

these miniatures belong to a different family from that of the Vatican and Paris sequences and enthuse about the authenticity of their gestures, claiming that 'the gestures and postures of F throughout show on the one hand more direct derivation from the antique original than do those of P and C, and on the other a Hellenistic mode in general';[24] and also that 'the review of the gestures has emphasized ... the superiority of F as representative of the archetypal illustration'.[25] This is far from being the view of the present writer,[26] although he accepts that cycles like this might have played a useful part in the transmission of gestures to later times. F is the only illustrated Terence to provide a miniature for *Heauton timorumenos* III, 3, v. 593.[27] It shows Chremes addressing Syrus. This miniature, however, has always created uncertainties since – despite the rules of oratory and the practice of characters in the Terence pictures – the figures here are gesturing with their left hands and not their right (pl. XLII*b*), although Jones and Morey have suggested that this was due to 'a reversal of the composition in the process of copying'.[28] Although we shall call upon this cycle in our final chapter, we shall not make use of it in the next stage of our investigation.

This is a system of internal analysis of a fairly elementary kind. In the manuscripts, the text of practically every scene is preceded by an illustration of it in a rectangular format extending across most of the width of the page and with the identifications of the characters written above. In the complete cycle of the six plays there are 144 such illustrations, and my argument is that, if a particular gesture being made by one of the characters portrayed can consistently be seen to relate to a given emotion being expressed by him in the text, then we may reasonably suppose that the gesture is there to indicate that particular state of mind. I would take as an example of this the gesture which, as I have

---

[24] J&M II, 199.   [25] *Ibid.*, p. 211.

[26] When we come to a detailed examination of the gestures, we shall realize that the gesture for compliance is misunderstood on four occasions in F and that for eavesdropping on three, that elsewhere gestures for acquiescence, love, forcefulness and puzzlement are also miscomprehended, that the gesture for surprise is converted to a simple pointing action, the gesture for pondering transformed into one for weeping, and the one for calm restraint into a fist. The resultant situation of a slave threatening his own master is one that common sense, let alone an understanding of the real gesture, should have precluded. And apart from all this, there are other discrepancies such as the fact that running figures are replaced by standing ones.

[27] F 36v, J&M I, no. 385.   [28] J&M II, 208.

remarked earlier, was mentioned by Quintilian who, we may recall, described it as follows: 'est et illa caua et rara et supra umeri altitudinem elata cum quodam motu uelut hortatrix manus.'[29]

FORCEFULNESS

In our illustrations, this gesture is used four times by one of the two brothers in the play named after them (*Adelphoe*), a play which is largely concerned with the conflicting temperaments and philosophies of them both. Demea is someone who is quick to anger and a great believer in the necessity of bringing up his son as strictly as possible. Micio, on the other hand, is easygoing and anxious to be relaxed in his behaviour to his adopted son in whom Demea takes an interest because he is, in fact, the real father of the boy. All this leads to occasions for friction and, on four of them, when Demea is at his most irascible, he has recourse to this gesture.

The first is in the second scene of Act I[30] when he is fulminating against the shameless activities of Micio's son in breaking into a household, and abducting a young woman from there (pl. XVI*a*). He then turns to Micio and puts all the primary blame for this on him. The latter's gentle defence seems to infuriate him further and provokes him to the remark that his brother is driving him mad: 'pro Iuppiter, tu homo adigi' me ad insaniam!'[31] It is clear from the strength of his language that he is losing control of himself, a fact to which Micio refers twice: once when he wishes to know if he is losing his temper ('irascere?', v. 136) and again when he asks himself whether, if he increased or even shared Demea's anger, this would not simply mean the provision of another madman:

> uerum si augeam
> aut etiam adiutor sim eius iracundiae,
> insaniam profecto cum illo.[32]

When other scandals associated with the young man reach Demea's

---

[29] XI.iii.103 (ed. Radermacher II, 347): 'there is also that gesture in which the hand is hollowed, with the fingers spread, and raised above the shoulder with a motion suggestive of exhortation.' See above, p. 24.

[30] P 99r, C 52r, J&M I, nos. 460–1.

[31] *Adelphoe* 111: 'By heaven, man, you're driving me insane!'   [32] *Adelphoe* 145–7.

ears (IV, 7),[33] they raise his blood-pressure again, and he is so galled by the philosophical reaction displayed by his brother to the misfortune related here, and then enlarged on further, that he turns on him again and resorts to sarcasm of an offensive kind, suggesting that Micio is presumably now ready to take up dancing and singing with the wife and mistress of his own son (vv. 750–2). His temper is as short as his language is strong and Micio has to tell him to abate it:

> iam uero omitte, Demea,
> tuam istanc iracundiam.[34]

Even so, he gives vent to it again when he is led to believe that his own son had been corrupted by Micio's, and he opens scene 3 of Act V[35] with the frenzied cry:

> ei mihi! quid faciam? quid agam? quid clamem aut querar?
> o caelum, o terra, o maria Neptuni![36]

On seeing Micio, he censures and upbraids him again, and the latter has once more to take it upon himself to advise his brother to curb his wrath: 'reprime iracundiam.'[37] Of this, the audience itelf gets a taste in Act IV, scene 6,[38] which Demea fills with an account of his recent trials. He tells them of how he had been trudging around the town on a wild goose chase instigated by a slave whom he roundly curses:

> ut, Syre, te cum tua
> monstratione magnu' perdat Iuppiter![39]

The major concern of *Phormio* is that, contrary to his father Demipho's plans for another arrangement, Antipho has fallen in love with, and married, a young woman during Demipho's absence. In taking this action, Antipho has enlisted the support of an intriguer, Phormio, who, with the help of Demipho's own slave, Geta, is anxious to outwit Demipho on his return. Demipho, like Demea, is in a bad mood when he

---

[33] P 116v, C 60v (where the gesture is misunderstood), J&M I, nos. 539–40.
[34] *Adelphoe* 754–5: 'Drop your ill temper now, Demea.'
[35] P 118v, C 61v, J&M I, nos. 553–4.
[36] *Adelphoe* 789–90: 'Great God, what shall I do? How shall I act? What cries and lamentations are enough? O Heaven and earth and Neptune's ocean!'
[37] *Adelphoe* 794.   [38] P 116r, C 60v, J&M I, nos. 534–5.
[39] *Adelphoe* 713–14: 'May the great Lord damn you, Syrus, for your directions!'

gives this gesture in the illustration to Act II, scene 3 of the play,[40] and the moment he comes on stage he expresses feelings of outrage:

> Enumquam quoiquam contumeliosius
> audisti' factam iniuriam quam haec est mihi?[41]

Geta comments both here (v. 350) and elsewhere (v. 426) that Demipho is in a temper, and Phormio says that he will work him up further (v. 351) which he very successfully does. Indeed, the scene is an object lesson in how a calculating schemer can incense someone by deliberate shafts of provocation, such as the gibe that Demipho is refusing to acknowledge his kinship with a person (who is, in fact, non-existent) because he thinks there would be no money in it for himself. If there were, Phormio goes on, the old man would soon have the identity of his grandfather's grandfather at his finger-tips. All this, of course, has its intended effect on Demipho as we see from one or two of his choleric comments and, not least, his explosive injunction to the gods to curse the man in front of him: 'di tibi malefaciant!'[42]

So far, strong language and anger seem to be necessary concomitants of this gesture. However, when we examine the contexts in which it is used elsewhere, we shall find that anger itself is not a necessary ingredient. Chremes, for example, in *Heauton timorumenos* is not an irascible person, indeed he refers to his own easygoing temperament, 'mea facilitas'.[43] Yet he can certainly be forceful and, according to the miniatures, he finds this gesture a useful reinforcement of that state on three occasions. One, in Act IV, scene 1,[44] is when he is inveighing against his wife for her disobedience to him at an earlier stage of their life. She had not carried out his instructions to expose a baby girl, a child who now seems to have reappeared in their lives as a young woman, and had compounded her offence, as he pointedly tells her, by her pretence that she had in fact done so, and by her failure to realize that she had put the child itself at risk since it could easily have found its way into the slave market. Another occasion (pl. XVI*b*) is when there is a more evenly balanced dispute

---

[40] P 157v, C 81v (where, as in F, the character is wrongly identified as Phormio), J&M I, nos. 714–15.

[41] *Phormio* 348–9: 'Have you ever heard of a wrongdoing more insolently done to anyone than this one to me?'

[42] *Phormio* 394.   [43] *Heauton timorumenos* 648.

[44] P 82v, C 43r, J&M I, nos. 386–7.

between the two since, on this occasion, his wife has begun by criticizing him (V, 3).[45] This was over the way he was treating his son which, she claimed, had led the latter to doubt his own parentage. Chremes' rejoinders are very strongly worded indeed, and include the tart response that the identity of the boy's mother is clear enough from the faults he shares with her. A third occasion (IV, 8)[46] is when, on hearing from Menedemus that the latter's son would like to marry his daughter, Chremes snaps out 'quaeso quid tu homini's?'[47] before going on to remind Menedemus of what he seems already to have forgotten, namely their earlier arrangements.

Phormio, also, is in no angry mood when he resorts to this gesture in Act V, scene 9 of the play named after him.[48] Following an altercation, he has decided in the most calculating of ways to expose Chremes to his own wife within her own home, and the old man is so frightened that he is described as being almost dead with fear. Despite some interruptions, which Phormio simply brushes aside, he makes unerringly for his main objective. This is to reveal the long-kept secret of Chremes that, over the years, he has maintained another household. It is a forceful performance which Phormio himself seems to see as a kind of duel (a very unequal one in this case), for he concludes by offering a challenge to anyone else who wishes to test his skill. Then, at the end of it all, as if to underline his commanding position, he coolly arranges for himself to be invited to an immediate dinner with the family whose tranquillity he has just destroyed.

The slave Parmeno, in *Eunuchus*, is of a very different class and character from those of Phormio, but there comes a time when he needs some of the latter's obduracy and calculation. This is when he feels the need to defend the interests of his master in the course of his love affair, and it may be of relevance to remind ourselves here that in the play *Aulularia* attributed to Plautus, the slave of Lyconides ruminates on the fact that it is the duty of one of his class to restrain an amorous master from precipitate action.[49] In the very first scene of the Terence play, Parmeno has seen the wretchedness caused to Phaedria by his uncertainties about the real feelings of his

---

[45] P 93r, C 49r, J&M I, nos. 433–4.   [46] P 89r, C 46v, J&M I, nos. 421–2.

[47] *Heauton timorumenos* 848: 'What kind of man are you?'

[48] P 174v, C 91r (where the gesture is misunderstood), J&M I, nos. 794–5.

[49] *Aulularia* 592–8.

mistress. At that time, he had counselled him against betraying the real intensity of his passion lest she exploit it, but now, in the ensuing scene (I, 2),[50] he sees Phaedria becoming agitated at her very appearance, weakening, and even trembling. In his anxiety to see that she shall not inveigle his master further while he is in his present state, he decides to examine her every statement quite mercilessly. When she tries to explain why she had refused her lover entrance, he sardonically retorts that it was, of course, because of love, and as she goes on, he monitors her pronounce-ments, accepting some but refuting others – her claims that she had had only one admirer to whom she owed all her wealth, and that she had made Phaedria her confidant in all things. Parmeno's manner is emphatic and peremptory and this hand-signal seems to be associated with the trenchancy of his comments, comments which the lady herself tries in vain to suppress.

In all these situations, the gesture is being used by someone who is being forceful or emphatic, and we might deduce that this is the meaning of the action. Indeed, if we apply this significance to it wherever it apears in our illustrations, it does seem to make good sense. In oratorical circles the same gesture, according to Quintilian, indicated exhortation, that is, forcefulness of speech. Now this agrees closely with the meaning we have deduced for the gesture from our own investigation, and the reader may think that this will both ratify our own interpretation of the gesture and validate our method of internal analysis for eliciting the meanings of other gestures in the Terence illustrations. We shall only add that this particular one has changed its meaning over the years. Whereas in Roman times it indicated forcefulness for both the actor and the orator, today it is something quite different: a courteous signal of parting among friends for, after all, the same hollowing of the hand and waving it over the head is our means of saying 'Goodbye' – 'God be with you' – to those we are fond of.

RESTRAINT

Micio is pilloried a good deal by his brother, but he does not submit to all this in a merely docile way. Even on the first occasion of being browbeaten about his son's behaviour, he ends up by simply telling

---

[50] P 37r, C 20r, J&M I, nos. 172–3.

Demea to refrain from harping on the theme and give him a chance to speak himself: 'ausculta, ne me optundas de hac re saepius.'[51] At the same time, according to the illustration,[52] he presents a gesture which consists of placing the hand at the level of the shoulders with the curved palm facing outwards, almost as if he is physically trying to ward something off. This action is here being used to restrain something and it is used as such elsewhere. So, Demea applies the same gesture to Micio himself when, towards the end of the play (V, 8),[53] he wishes to calm down the latter's anxieties about the energetic attempts being made to persuade him to marry the widowed lady, Sostrata; Micio is desperately protesting that he wants to be left alone, and that his tormentor must be out of his mind to suppose that he will be willing, in his sixty-fifth year, to become the bridegroom of a broken down old woman:

> satin sanus es?
> ego nouo' maritus anno demum quinto et sexagensumo
> fiam atque anum decrepitam ducam?[54]

And Demea calls on the gesture again when he is being told by Hegio that the youth he has complained about so bitterly has reached a new level of villainy – he has ravished a neighbour's daughter (III, 4). But this is not all. Hegio goes on to say that there is yet worse to follow, and at this point Demea asks if such is possible: 'an quid est etiam amplius?'[55] The positioning of his hand[56] reinforces his anxiety to hold back further revelations (pl. XVII*a*).

Chremes utilizes this hand-signal in *Andria* (III, 3)[57] when trying to fight off the importunities of Simo. Indeed, the latter is pressurizing him so much to continue with their original plan of joining their offspring together in matrimony that he is driven to declare:

---

[51] *Adelphoe* 113: 'Just listen, instead of perpetually hammering away at me on this matter.'

[52] P 99r (J&M I, no. 460) misunderstands the gesture and raises it high enough for it to become a gesture for forcefulness. It is correct in C 52r (J&M I, no. 461).

[53] P 122v, C 63v, J&M I, nos. 572–3.

[54] *Adelphoe* 937–9: 'Are you in your right mind? I become a bridegroom in my sixty-fifth year and take as wife a decrepit old crone?'

[55] *Adelphoe* 468: 'Can there be anything more?'

[56] P 109r, C 57r, J&M I, nos. 504–5.   [57] P 19v, C 11v, J&M I, nos. 97–8.

ah ne me obsecra:
quasi hoc te orando a me impetrare oporteat.[58]

In the same way, the youth Clitipho has recourse to it, too. This is in *Heauton timorumenos* III, 3,[59] when he is anxious to stay the reproaches of the slave Syrus. The young man has been censured by his father for the degree of intimacy he has shown towards Bacchis, which his father holds to be unmannerly. Syrus also takes exception to it but for a different reason: namely that it is injudicious and he fears that this kind of conduct will betray the plans he has for securing money from Chremes' neighbour, Menedemus. Clitipho, who is willing to take advantage of the slave's guile, is not so prepared to listen to his implied criticism and he cuts him off brusquely with an order to be quiet: 'tace sodes'.[60]

In *Phormio* (II, 1), it is not so much a question of a youth making this gesture to a slave, as of a youth and a slave enlisting it together.[61] By cajolery and their own edited version of events, Phaedria and Geta are in the process of trying to hold back the verbal attacks being made on them by Demipho, who is furious with them for allowing his son to marry without his consent. He himself will be driven to adopt the gesture later, though then in support of his brother, Chremes, who has even more need of it in one of the great crises of his life. This is when, in Act V, scene 9, Phormio is about to disclose to his wife the sorry story of his prolonged infidelity and he is prepared to go to any lengths to stop him. 'Caue isti quicquam creduas', he calls to his wife,[62] and to Phormio himself, 'non taces?'[63] In the event, neither his words nor this gesture are of avail and, in the related picture,[64] Demipho is directing the gesture to Phormio and Chremes to his wife, whose questions he is anxious to suppress.

On one occasion, the gesture is used not simply to stop, but to interdict a statement. This is when, in Act V, scene 4 of *Hecyra*, Pamphilus meets Bacchis after a happy resolution of his marital problems, a resolution which, incidentally, reflects little credit on himself. On discovering that she has kept silence to his father about the true facts of the matter, he asks her to continue to say nothing (v. 866) to the

---

[58] *Andria* 543–4: 'Don't entreat me: pleading is not a way of getting my consent.'
[59] P 81v, C 42v, J&M I, nos. 380–1.   [60] *Heauton timorumenos* 580.
[61] P 154v, C 80r, J&M I, nos. 704–5.
[62] *Phormio* 993: 'Don't believe anything he says!'
[63] *Phormio* 987: 'Won't you be quiet?'   [64] P 174v, C 91r, J&M I, nos. 794–5.

accompaniment of this gesture,[65] following it up with the well-known dig at the traditions of the play-writing profession: namely that he does not want everyone to get to know everything here as they do in comedies. As we have seen, however, more usually the gesture is used to inhibit speech, and as such, it is employed by both Pamphilus and his father at different stages of this play. By Pamphilus, according to the Paris manuscript, to restrain the objections and complaints of Parmeno about the errand he has been sent on in Act III, scene 4;[66] by Laches, who wishes Bacchis to put a stop to her interruptions and allow him to continue with his own remarks, in Act V, scene 1.[67]

When embarrassed by his brother's excessive praise of him in *Adelphoe* (II, 4), Aeschinus finds in this action[68] a useful endorsement of his views that the other should make a halt to this kind of flattery. His reproof is a mild one – 'age inepte, quasi nunc non norimu' nos inter nos'[69] – but the gesture adds strength to it. Then Thais, in *Eunuchus* (V, 2),[70] finds it a convenient adjunct to the more lenient view she has decided to take of Chaerea's behaviour (vv. 878–80). This leads her to grant him the pardon for which he has been pleading for having disrupted her household, and her gesture (pl. XXIX*b*) tells him that he can now be quiet since all is forgiven. And she has much to forgive, for he has been guilty of gross deception and seduction. Having seen a young woman of her household with whom he has become infatuated, he has made arrangements to exchange places and attire with a eunuch who has just been presented to Thais, and in this guise, to gain access to her home where he has deflowered the woman concerned. The seriousness of the action was compounded by the fact that the girl was under the special protection of Thais. The latter had recovered her from slavery in order to restore her to the family from which she had been kidnapped, a family which happened to be that of Thais' own lover. Again, when the real eunuch has been apprehended in the mistaken belief that he was the

---

[65] P 146v, C 76r, J&M I, nos. 673–4.

[66] P 136r, C 70v (where, however, Pamphilus simply has the gesture for speech), J&M I, nos. 628–9.

[67] P 143v, C 74v, J&M I, nos. 658–9.

[68] P 103v (where the gesture is misunderstood), C 54v, J&M I, nos. 480–1.

[69] *Adelphoe* 271: 'Come, you silly fellow: surely we know each other by now.'

[70] P 58v, C 30v, J&M I, nos. 269–70.

culprit, Phaedria gives this gesture to him to quieten his protests (*Eunuchus* IV, 4).[71]

The gesture which accompanies efforts to restrain speech in our miniatures is also associated with attempts to inhibit actions, intended actions, and even feelings, and an example of the first is to be found in the illustration to *Adelphoe* IV, 2.[72] Here Ctesipho is anxious to ward off retribution in the shape of his father whose entry he is trying to prevent, and he finds this a useful reinforcement of his cry to Syrus: 'obsecro uide ne ille huc prorsu' se inruat.'[73]

Elsewhere, the gesture is deemed appropriate by Chremes when he is trying to hold Menedemus back from an impetuous decision concerning his son in a situation that we shall refer to later (*Heauton timorumenos* III, 1).[74] Again, Demipho makes use of it in *Phormio*[75] when he is trying to stop something happening (pl. XVII*b*). This is the attempt by Chremes to involve his wife in their plans and to get her to carry information about them to the woman that his (Demipho's) son has married (IV, 5, vv. 718–27). In fact, however, he has already been pre-empted in this.

The gesture that can be used by one man to stop the intentions of another is in one instance adopted by a character to stay his own. This is in the illustration to Act IV, scene 5 of *Andria*.[76] On learning of the death of a relative to whose estate he has a just claim, Crito journeys to the relevant area only to discover that a young woman, considered to be the sister of the deceased, is already in possession of the property. For this and other reasons, he believes that it would be best for him to hold back from his original intention and to return home (vv. 806–16), and although his thoughts are spoken aloud to a servant, they are, like the accompanying gesture, really addressed to himself.

On the three occasions when Pamphilus makes this gesture to his

[71] P 53v, C 27v, J&M I, nos. 244–5. Phaedria and the eunuch are mislabelled in terms of each other.

[72] P 111v, C 58r, J&M I, nos. 514–15.

[73] *Adelphoe* 550: 'For heaven's sake, don't let him dash right in here!'

[74] P 78r, C 41r, J&M I, nos. 368–9.

[75] P, on 167r (J&M I, no. 757), correctly shows Demipho making this gesture although C, on 86v (J&M I, no. 758), gives it to Chremes and has Demipho with the *adlocutio* gesture. We know that P is here in the right both because the text demands it and because Demipho is carrying the money which he should according to lines 712 and 715.

[76] P 28r, C 15v, J&M I, nos. 137–8.

parents in *Hecyra*, it is associated with a desire to hold them back from something, and to understand this, we shall need to give a brief account of the main plot of the play. On returning from abroad, Pamphilus is told that there have been differences between his wife and his mother as a result of which his wife has left the house she shares with his parents and returned to her own parental home. He later, however, learns of the true facts of the matter which are that, as the result of an assault by a stranger, his wife has been made pregnant and she has left her marital home in order to conceal her condition. Not even her own father knows of this and only her mother shares her secret. The latter implores Pamphilus not to divulge it, which he agrees to do, but this does not mean that he will take the wronged lady back. When, therefore, in Act III, scene 5, his father, in company with his father-in-law, visits him and asks him to recall her, he feels it necessary to put a stop to any such hopes with this gesture and with the words 'non est consilium, pater'.[77] At a later meeting with both his parents (IV, 3),[78] he makes it clear by the same gesture that he wishes to put an end to his father's continuing hopes that he will change his mind, and he comments: 'sed non minuam meum consilium: ex usu quod est id persequar.'[79] At the same time, he lets his mother know that he does not wish her to go into the country as she plans, believing as she does that this will help restore harmony to his marriage (vv. 612–14). On the third occasion that he displays the gesture, it is when he is trying to quell his mother's anxieties about the supposed illness of his wife (III, 2, vv. 355–7).[80]

At one point in *Eunuchus* (III, 3), Chremes claims, like Pamphilus' mother, that he is going to the country although for a less serious reason. He is merely using it as an excuse for his decision to refuse Thais' pressing invitation that he should visit her, and he reinforces his refusal by a display of this gesture to her messenger.[81] Later (IV, 6),[82] he has recourse to it again when rejecting another communication of hers, although now of a less complimentary sort. It is when she sees how he reacts to the information that the soldier Thraso will soon appear with his troop and

---

[77] *Hecyra* 494: 'That is not my purpose, father.' P 137r, C 71r, J&M I, nos. 633–4.
[78] P 140v, C 73r, J&M I, nos. 648–9.
[79] *Hecyra* 616: 'I shall not alter my resolve and shall follow the course that is best.'
[80] P 134r, C 69v, J&M I, nos. 618–19.
[81] P 48r, C 25r, J&M I, nos. 209–10.   [82] P 55v, C 29r, J&M I, nos. 254–5.

suggests that this is making him nervous, a charge that he wishes to refute.

This is a gesture that appears twenty-two times in our miniatures, helping to illustrate all the six plays of Terence. It finds a place in every kind of situation – hostile, friendly, curt and cautious – and in exchanges between persons in all kinds of relationship – a master to a slave and a slave to a master, a eunuch to a youth and a lady to a suppliant, a son to a mother and a man to a brother, a neighbour, an enemy and a friend. In all this, there is a consistency of meaning – a desire to check or hold something back, whether it be the comments, or actions, or intentions of another, and we can therefore call it the gesture of restraint.

BELLIGERENCE

When Phaedria and Geta together make this gesture to Demipho in Act II, scene 1 of *Phormio*,[83] they have more than his verbal abuse to contend with, for the brandishing of his fist (pl. XVIII*a*) shows that he is threatening physical violence as well. This indication of hostility is found in Plautus[84] and is described by Bulwer, whom we have referred to earlier, and who rightly says that it is a plain indication of aggression,[85] illustrating it with a drawing which is labelled succinctly enough as *Minor* ('I threaten').[86] The gesture is hardly one that calls for explanation although we may find it unusual to see it used in our illustrations by a woman. This is Thais in Act V, scene 1 of *Eunuchus*[87] when she is furiously admonishing a servant (pl. XVIII*b*). Unlike the male slave Geta, the female one here does not try to restrain the belligerence being offered her by the gesture, but uses another gesture which, unlike the confronting fist, is very much in need of elucidation.

If, today, we saw someone approaching with the backs of his first and middle fingers held up towards us, we would not be too well pleased. In our present culture it is an offensive action: it is an affront. This was not, however, true at the time when the original Terence miniatures were made, and this we shall see if we examine all the examples they yield of

[83] P 154v, C 80r, J&M I, nos. 704–5. [84] *Amphitruo* 302–23 and *Cistellaria* 235.
[85] Bulwer, *Chirologia*, p. 57. [86] *Ibid.*, illustration Y in the table on p. 151.
[87] P 57v, C 30r, J&M I, nos. 264–5.

its use, beginning with a character we have already encountered, Menedemus.

COMPLIANCE, CONCILIATION

Menedemus is the 'self-tormentor' alluded to in the title of the play *Heauton timorumenos*. His harsh discipline has forced his son to leave the parental home and seek refuge in exile abroad, but Menedemus is then so eaten up with remorse that he spends his days in the self-inflicted penance of taking over the tasks normally performed by slaves and working the lands of his estate with his own hands. In Act III, scene 1, it is the happy lot of his kindly neighbour, Chremes, to report to him the joyful news that his son has finally returned, but also to warn him not to follow his impetuous intention and give him, when he comes back, everything he desires, thus extending to him a generosity that would be as excessive as his former parsimony. This, says Chremes, would be doing the young man a great disservice; it would encourage him in profligacy and undermine his character. Menedemus not only agrees to accept this helpful advice, but after learning that his companion has lost a night's sleep reflecting on his problem, offers him his hand in friendship (v. 493). The two-fingered gesture which he gives in the illustration (pl. XIX*a*)[88] cannot, then, be an expresssion of insulting derision as it would be today. Nor the same gesture that a son makes to his father to whom he is declaring his subjection in quite abject terms. This is in Act V, scene 3 of *Andria*.[89] The father has been berating him for claiming that his mistress is an Athenian (and thereby thwarting the parental plan for him to marry another) and in the process tells the boy in no uncertain terms that he is shameless, disobedient, manipulative, and prepared to break his father's heart. After these strictures, and with only one reservation, Pamphilus yields in terms that are every bit as extreme in their expression as those he has just heard:

> ego me amare hanc fateor; si id peccarest, fateor id quoque.
> tibi, pater, me dedo: quiduis oneris inpone, impera.
> uis me uxorem ducere? hanc uis amittere? ut potero feram.[90]

---

[88] P 78r, C 41r, J&M I, nos. 368–9.   [89] P 31r, C 17r, J&M I, nos. 148–9.

[90] *Andria* 896–8: 'I confess I love her and if that is a fault, I admit it. I put myself,

We can hardly suppose that his accompanying gesture was intended to offer a slight. Nor the same one used by another youth in another play when he is begging for his mother's help.[91] The idea has been put into Clitipho's head that his father had suddenly turned against him because he was not, as he had always believed, that father's son and he is plaintively asking his mother whether this is so or not:

> si umquam ullum fuit tempu', mater, quom ego uoluptati tibi
> fuerim, dictu' filiu' tuo' uostra uoluntate, obsecro
> eius ut memineris atque inopi' nunc te miserescat mei,
> quod peto aut quod uolo, parentes meos ut commonstres mihi.[92]

In *Eunuchus* (I, 2), yet another youth gives the same hand-signal to his mistress.[93] He has reluctantly agreed to stay away from her for two days despite the fact that he is aware that, during that time, she will be in touch with his rival, the military officer. He is desperately anxious that she will keep faith with him during his absence and is urgently pleading for her loyalty:

> cum milite istoc praesens absens ut sies;
> dies noctesque me ames, me desideres,
> me somnies, me exspectes, de me cogites,
> me speres, me te oblectes, mecum tota sis:
> meu' fac sis postremo animu' quando ego sum tuos.[94]

It is not likely that, as he says this with his lips, he will be registering contempt with his hand.

Thais, the lady who is the subject of these protestations, appears in a less amorous setting in a later scene of the play (V, 1) when she is shown upbraiding one of her servants, as we saw at the beginning of our account of this gesture. She has discovered that, during her absence, the girl she

father, in your hands. Put any burden on me, give me your commands. Do you want me to take a wife? to dismiss my love? I will bear it as well as I can.'
91 P 93v, C 49r, J&M I, nos. 438–9.
92 *Heauton timorumenos* 1024–7: 'If ever there was a time, mother, when you delighted in me and it pleased you to call me your son, I implore you to remember it and have pity on my need: to hear from you who my parents are.'
93 P 37r, C 20r, J&M I, nos. 172–3.
94 *Eunuchus* 192–6: 'When you are with this soldier, be away from him: by day and night, love me, long for me, dream of me, wait for me, think of me, hope for me, delight in me, be wholly mine. Give me your heart entire as you have mine.'

has been cosseting has been ravished and misused and can now only weep in silence (v. 820). For this she blames her servant, Pythias, and for failing to protect her charge, for entrusting her sheep to the mercies of a wolf (as her mistress shouts at her), the slave is feeling the edge of the latter's tongue. The unfortunate wretch makes things even worse for herself by asserting that the villain concerned was the brother of her mistress' suitor. In such a context, we can hardly imagine that the two-fingered gesture with which the servant salutes the mistress in the related picture (pl. IX*a*)[95] is intended to display derision.

Another slave who finds a use for this gesture is Syrus in *Heauton timorumenos* (V, 2).[96] It is at a moment that, for him, is a particularly delicate one. He has just been the witness to his master disinheriting his son both because he disapproves of his behaviour and because he believes that any possessions that come into his hands will end up in those of his mistress. Syrus has now to pluck up enough courage to tell that master that he, the slave, is responsible for the offences for which he has so harshly punished the son. In fact, Syrus is on such tenterhooks that he even feels it necessary to ask if it is safe for him to speak at all (v. 973). Again, it is not probable that his gesture was intended to be an insulting one.

In Act IV, scene 4 of another play, *Phormio*, yet another slave, Geta, remarks that he has been cheating the old men of their cash – 'emunxi argento senes'[97] – and he has been shown doing just this in the previous scene.[98] There, he is seen wheedling money out of his master and the latter's brother on the specious promise of a marriage of convenience that Phormio will arrange for himself in order to disembarrass them of an earlier, and unlooked for, alliance. As with all confidence-tricksters – and Geta is here acting as an agent for one of them – he realizes that the amount he will gain will depend on the glibness of his tongue and smoothness of his demeanour, and he displays himself adept at both. He begins with a conversational approach, then presents himself as a man with an active mind who has been busily considering their problem, and next as a man of affairs who will negotiate (albeit uninvited) on behalf of the others. All this is seasoned with a little flattery which enables him to

---

[95] P 57v, C 30r, J&M I, nos. 264–5.

[96] P 90r (wrongly inserted here), C 48r, J&M I, nos. 426 and 431.

[97] *Phormio* 682.   [98] P 164r, C 85v, J&M I, nos. 747–8.

allude to the eloquence and the liberal ways of his master (vv. 623 and 629). It is hard to believe that the gesture he gives in these circumstances was intended to be an offensive one. In fact, the reverse is true as we shall see if we look back to the contexts in which this particular gesture has so far appeared.

In the first it was made by an elderly man to a neighbour, to whom he is beholden for having brought him the wonderful news of his son's return, for having lost a night's sleep worrying about his own problem, and for having saved him from a foolish decision. Indeed, before the scene is out, he marks his indebtedness to Chremes by insisting on clasping hands to consolidate their friendship. In the second, it was employed by a son who was capitulating to his father, and in the third by another son who is beseeching his mother for information vital to himself. It is true that this is followed by a highly critical outburst from his father but, if the scene begins with this son begging for his mother's help, it ends with him making it clear that he wishes he could placate his father (*Heauton timorumenos* 1044). In the fourth, it was displayed by a youth trying to find favour with his mistress, and in the fifth, by a female slave to an infuriated mistress, who opens the scene by telling her to stop making silly excuses and goes on to hurl abuse at her for her stupidity and neglect. In the sixth, it was exhibited by a male slave making an apprehensive approach to a master whose severity he has just had the opportunity to gauge. In the seventh, it was used by another slave, who was anxious to ingratiate himself with two elderly gentlemen, one of whom is his master. The common denominator of all these is not a wish to offend, but a desire to propitiate, and the gesture can best be described as that for compliance. Indeed, it is worth noting that, as Phaedria makes this particular gesture to his mistress in the relevant illustration, he is saying on stage that her wish must be carried out and that she must be gratified: 'faciundumst quod uis ... mos gerundust Thaidi.'[99] And we may add to this that, when Micio enters the stage by himself in Act I, scene 1 of *Adelphoe*,[100] he makes this gesture as he explains to the spectators that he has always been compliant in his attitudes to his son: compliant in financing him liberally, compliant in overlooking his misdemeanours, and compliant in the affectionate tolerance he has always extended to him.

---

[99] *Eunuchus* 186 and 188.   [100] P 97v, C 51v, J&M I, nos. 455–6.

Such a gesture of compliance Chremes finds appropriate for himself when, in *Andria* (III, 4),[101] he has decided to become more conciliatory to the wishes of his friend and allow his daughter to marry the latter's son despite certain complications. That friend twice remarks on the fact that he has had to overcome an earlier reluctance on the part of Chremes (vv. 592–3), whose present compliance finds final endorsement in his concluding remark that he is now going home to tell his daughter to make herself ready (v. 594).

We would expect a gesture of accommodation, such as this, to be much used by servants and slaves, and this is in fact what we find. Indeed, if we exclude the Prologue, the very first illustrated scene of the Vatican and Paris manuscripts (*Andria* I, 1) includes Sosia, now freed, but still a servant, who is making this gesture in the picture[102] while on the stage he is expressing gratitude to his master for the latter's approval, and saying that he will be glad to serve him in the future as in the past.[103] When he hears of his young master's anxiety to find the girl who has just swept him off his feet, it is also to the reinforcement of the same hand-signal that Parmeno, another slave in another play, tells Chaerea that he will be industrious, conscientious, and helpful on his master's behalf:

faciam sedulo ac
dabo operam, adiuuabo.[104]

The gesture is used by Davus in *Andria* (II, 6)[105] when giving his master information which, whatever its relationship to the facts, is what that master most wants to hear, namely that his son will not object to the parental marriage-plans for him despite his present entanglement with another woman; and by Dromo in the same play (V, 2) as he awaits the same master's instructions. Again, when Ctesipho enters scene 3 of Act II of *Adelphoe* in his search for his brother whom he is anxious to thank, he finds the slave Syrus all too ready to help him in his quest, and displaying this gesture (pl. XIX*b*).[106]

We have already seen that the slave Geta had recourse to it when trying to wheedle money out of his master and his master's brother, and he falls

---

[101] P 21r, C 12r, J&M I, nos. 103–4.   [102] P 6r, C 4v, J&M I, nos. 16–17.

[103] *Andria* 40–1.

[104] *Eunuchus* 362–3: 'I'll do my best, I'll work hard to help you.' P 42v, C 22v, J&M I, nos. 192–3.

[105] P 16v, C 10r, J&M I, nos. 77–8.   [106] P 103r, C 54r, J&M I, nos. 475–6.

back on it again when, in Act V, scene 2 of *Phormio* (vv. 766–75),[107] he particularly wants to show deference, not to say sycophancy, to his master by readily agreeing with everything he says. Demipho begins with the remark that it is because some want to appear honest that others are enabled to be rogues and that it is a pity he has parted with his own money. 'Planissime', replies Geta.[108] In these days, goes on the old man, it is those who debauch what is right who really profit, and the slave replies, 'uerissume'.[109] We have been foolish in this affair, continues Demipho, and the response to this is again conciliatory.

In point of fact, Geta is playing a double game. His sympathies are not with his master, but with his master's son, who – as we have seen – has married during his father's absence and without his consent, and Geta is supporting Phormio's efforts to help the son out of the quandary in which he has placed himself. The primary plan is to take advantage of an aspect of the law which insists that orphans be either married to, or portioned out by, their nearest relatives, and to claim that the son's bride falls within the kinship category. This, of course, is disputed by Demipho, and in scene 3 of Act II, he is shown with his three legal advisers confronting the practised intriguer. Geta sides with Phormio, who certainly treats him as an ally. So, on the old man's entry, they exchange comments about his mood (v. 350), and as time goes on, Phormio tells Geta when to respond to his master (v. 375), confides to him when he thinks his adversary is losing his nerve (v. 429), asks to be reminded of the name they had dreamed up for the kinsman of their imagination (v. 387), and at the end, asks to be advised when he is wanted again (v. 440). Geta, for his part, advises Phormio when to be cautious (v. 398), notifies him when he is doing well (v. 429), and comments when his master seems to be losing his temper (v. 426). But all this collusion must necessarily be surreptitious, and as far as the others are concerned, Geta has to put on a great show: a charade of supporting his master. So, for their benefit, he attacks and abuses Phormio (vv. 359, 372 and 374), sympathizes with Demipho for the insults being hurled at him (vv. 375–7), and at one point goes so far as to congratulate his master on one of his ripostes: 'eu noster.'[110] The fact that he is directing the gesture we are discussing towards his master in

---

[107] P 168v, C 87v, J&M I, nos. 767–8.   [108] *Phormio* 771: 'Clearly so.'

[109] *Phormio* 772: 'All too true.'   [110] *Phormio* 398: 'Well done, our side!'

the related miniature[111] is all part of this performance: the pretence that it is this person he is anxious to support and conciliate.

The gesture may be appropriate in the hands of slaves addressing their masters, but there are times when the position can be reversed.

Chremes finds this a convenient signal in *Heauton timorumenos* (IV, 5)[112] to indicate his own compliance with a subterfuge of Syrus, his slave, which he has himself encouraged. Although there is more to it than this, he had earlier suggested to the slave that Clitipho should be helped to extract money from his father in order to maintain his mistress, the idea being that the young man would thereby be persuaded to stay at the home from which he had earlier fled (vv. 533–5, 540 and 543–5). When Chremes sees a woman whom he believes to be the said mistress entering the house of Clitipho's father with all her baggage and attendants (IV, 4), he believes that Syrus has achieved what he himself has abetted, and not only gives this gesture but also, in the text, pats him on the head, adding the remark that he will be glad to do him a good turn when he can (vv. 761–3).

The most curious example of the master communicating with the slave in this way is in a scene in *Phormio* (IV, 3)[113] that we have already referred to, where Geta is presenting this indicator as he hopes to get as much money as possible from his master, Demipho (pl. XXIX*a*). Demipho responds with the same gesture, and this is because he is equally anxious to secure Geta's goodwill since on him rests his only hope of getting his son, Antipho, released from his ill-advised marriage. Later in the same play (V, 6), the same son gives the same gesture to the same slave,[114] and this is to indicate his collusion with Geta's act of disloyalty to his father which has enabled him to discover the latter's most treasured secret and, with it, the key to Antipho's own future happiness. Indeed, he can now describe himself as being beloved of the gods, soaked through with delight. Antipho's use of this gesture to the same slave in an earlier part of the play (IV, 4)[115] is more difficult to explain, but usually its interpretation is straightforward enough.

Not that it necessarily has to be in response to the text, for it can be used when it is simply appropriate to the situation, as we see in the

---

[111] P 157v, C 81v, J&M I, nos. 714–15.   [112] P 86v, C 45v, J&M I, nos. 406–7.

[113] P 164r, C 85v, J&M I, nos. 747–8.   [114] P 171r, C 89r, J&M I, nos. 787–8.

[115] P 166r, C 86r, J&M I, nos. 752–3.

illustration of the second scene of Act III of *Hecyra*.[116] Here, the slave finds himself in the unfortunate position of having to tell his master's mother for a second time that she will not be allowed to enter the sickroom of her daughter-in-law. This is an apparently unfriendly message but, by using this deferential salutation, the slave is able to dissociate himself from the decision itself, a posture which is not authorized by the text but which could easily happen in an acting situation.

The same gesture had been used by his own master at an earlier stage of the action. This was when he, too, was confronted with an embarrassing situation. As we have seen, Pamphilus had agreed to his mother-in-law's agitated request not to divulge the secret of his wife's pregnancy, but, once the child is born, he can neither accept it as his own nor divulge the reason why, and his excuse (which ironically happens to reflect the truth) is that he had not been informed of the pregnancy in the first place. On the surface, it is obviously a very flimsy one. We have referred to an earlier visit paid on him by his father and father-in-law, and now that an infant has appeared, they make another, still in ignorance of the true situation, and therefore quite willing to confront him with what they consider to be his shilly-shallying (IV, 4). The father-in-law, as he himself says, remains anxious to keep on good terms with the young man, but the father is enraged by his lack of concern, which he attributes to his son's more pressing interest in a mistress, and he angrily demands that he take in the mother and child, or at least the child. Despite all these strictures, Pamphilus firmly keeps to his resolve not to allow either of them into his home. Yet, the fact that, at the same time, he is presenting this gesture to his father[117] will indicate that, however regrettable the differences between them, he is still anxious to show a spirit of conciliation. This, again, could well come naturally on the stage although it is not specifically suggested by the spoken words.

As it happens, Pamphilus had had this same gesture presented to him by his slave on an earlier occasion. On his first re-entry into his own home after leaving the harbour, the young man is told of differences between his wife and mother and he fills the stage with lamentations about the fact that he has ever returned at all (III, 1).[118] His slave, Parmeno, strives

116 P 134r, C 69v, J&M I, nos. 618–19. 117 P 141r, C 73v, J&M I, nos. 653–4.
118 P 132v, C 69r, J&M I, nos. 613–14.

hard to soothe his agitated spirits by telling him that, if he had stayed away longer, the resentment between the two women might have become worse, and that now he is back he can look into the cause of it all and perhaps find it to be only a minor problem which can easily be resolved. Pamphilus himself refers to these ministrations as being efforts to comfort him – 'quid consolare me?'[119] – but perhaps the word 'mollify' would be a more appropriate one.

And it may be in this spirit of mollification that another slave makes this gesture to another character who has been distressing himself: not, like Pamphilus, over his return home, but over his rapid exit from it. Antipho, in *Phormio*, has fled from his father out of fear of the latter's wrath at his having married without parental consent, and in Act III, scene 1, he castigates himself for his cowardice. The slave Geta tries to solace him and relieve his anxieties by assuring him that his father is unaware of the real situation and that the position is under control, all to the accompaniment of our present gesture.[120] It is one that is used again by yet another slave to yet another anguished master in a relationship that we have already seen – that of Parmeno to Phaedria. Phaedria's indecision towards his mistress we have earlier remarked on, and his slave's reactions to his distracted comments give him an opportunity to use the gesture under discussion (*Eunuchus* I, 1).[121] The slave advises his master not to commit himself in any direction while he is in an unsettled and angry mood. If he can keep to his resolve to stay away, the servant says, then that will be excellent, but if he cannot, then Thais will perceive what a hold she has over her lover and he will certainly be at her mercy. A further outburst from Phaedria is followed by more advice from the slave clearly aimed to assuage the feelings of his master and persuade him to make the best of his lot. Perhaps, in this context again, the gesture is there to indicate mollification.

Not that this idea of mollification is far removed from that of compliance which remains the basic significance of the gesture, whatever slight nuances of meaning it may carry as well. It is, indeed, an interpretation which may have some relevance to a similar gesture which appears in classical art in a carving which, like the originals of our miniatures, can be attributed to the third century AD. It is that of a

---

[119] *Hecyra* 293: 'Why try to comfort me?'   [120] P 160r, C 83r, J&M I, nos. 723–4.
[121] P 36r, C 19v, J&M I, nos. 167–8.

poet – or of someone affecting to be one – on a sarcophagus, now in Vienna.[122] He is addressing his Muse with a gesture which Wegner simply describes as an oratorical one,[123] but which – despite the fact that the thumb is laid across the palm instead of aligning itself to the forefinger as in the Terence – is very similar to the one we have been discussing. A comparable gesture is also made by another poet (once claimed on somewhat fragile evidence to be Homer) in the carvings of an earlier sarcophagus in the Louvre.[124] If we apply to the gesture here the meaning that we have assigned to the analogous one in the Terence illustrations, then it would have a certain appropriateness since we would expect a poet's attitude towards his Muse to be one of compliance.

The only occasion on which a father uses this gesture of compliance to a son is in the illustration to Act I, scene 2 of *Heauton timorumenos*.[125] The father is Chremes who, at the opening of the play, is shown listening to the sad story of his neighbour Menedemus, which we have recounted above, and there are tears in his eyes on the latter's departure. Before this, Chremes had tried to console his neighbour with the thought that his son will probably come back soon. Chremes is amazed when, in the next scene, he is met at the door by his own son, Clitipho, with the news that the other's son has indeed returned, and been welcomed at the port and entertained by himself. The father is naturally delighted, and his indication of compliance with the hospitable attitude of Clitipho is an understandable one. Clitipho, on his part, however, cannot concur with an early statement of his father's that Menedemus' son is still in Asia for he has only just been talking to him, and he indicates his divergence of opinion by lowering his arm obliquely from the shoulder and turning the palm away from the person being addressed (pl. XX*a*).[126] This is the signal for dissent.

---

122 Kunsthistorisches Museum, Antikensammlung, Inv. I 1117. See Wegner, *Die Musensarkophage*, pp. 89–90 (no. 230) and pl. 127a. The figure of the poet is at the right-hand end of the relief.

123 *Ibid.*, p. 89.

124 Paris, Musée du Louvre, Ma 475. See Baratte and Metzger, *Catalogue des sarcophages en pierre d'époques romaine et paléochrétienne*, no. 84 and pl. on p. 174.

125 P 71v, C 37v, J&M I, nos. 337–8.   126 *Ibid.*

DISSENT

We find it therefore being used by the maid in Act I, scene 4 of *Andria* (pl. XX*b*)[127] as she declares her disagreement with the choice of the midwife she has been asked to summon since, in her view, the latter is too careless on the one hand, and too interested in drink on the other. In a later part of the action (V, 4) it is used to signify dissent again.[128] This time by Crito, a citizen of Andros, when he brushes aside the disbelieving and scornful comments of Simo against his testimony of the free birth of the girl from Andros, knowing for certain that his statements are correct:

> si mihi perget quae uolt dicere, ea quae non uolt audiet . . .
> nam ego quae dico uera an falsa audierim iam sciri potest.[129]

Crito then embarks on his detailed account of the birth.

This last gesture is unknown to us today. Another – that for forcefulness – has changed its meaning over the years. Yet another – that for compliance – has completely reversed its. However, there is a gesture in our Terence repertory which means today exactly what it did on the Roman stage in the third century. It is the joining together of the thumb and forefinger to form a circle while the other fingers are outstretched. Then, as now, it signified agreement or acquiescence.

AGREEMENT, APPROVAL

Laches, whom we have seen making the signal for eavesdropping in one scene of *Hecyra*, appears in the next (IV, 3) displaying this particular gesture (pl. XXI*a*).[130] It is clearly to indicate that he agrees with everything he has overheard his wife say to their son about going into the country in order to relieve pressures on his marriage, for, after observing that it is better to make a decision now than to be forced into it later, he tells her to get ready to leave immediately. Hegio adopts the same gesture when, in Act III, scene 4 of *Adelphoe*,[131] he agrees to Geta's plea that he should succour the slave's mistress, telling the suppliant that he should not even voice the thought of him not giving his help; he cannot do

---

[127] P 9r, C 6v, J&M I, nos. 34–5.   [128] P 32r, C 17v, J&M I, nos. 154–5.

[129] *Andria* 920–2: 'If he goes on telling me what he wants, he will hear what he doesn't want . . . We can soon see whether what I was told is true or false.'

[130] P 140v, C 73r, J&M I, nos. 648–9.   [131] P 109r, C 57r, J&M I, nos. 504–5.

enough when duty calls (vv. 458–9). As it happens, he is able to act on this compliance with something like the alacrity of Laches since the very person whom he must approach on the subject soon walks up to him.

We have already had occasion to refer to the bargaining between Geta and Demipho in Act IV, scene 3 of *Phormio* over the price to be paid for marrying off Antipho's present wife, where each presents the gesture for compliance for reasons of his own. Chremes, in the meantime, gives our present gesture for agreement (pl. XXIX*a*) which marks the different attitudes of the two brothers. Demipho is indeed initially anxious to accommodate the slave in the arrangements he is making and agrees to the stated terms. But, as the price rises higher and higher because of the supposed needs of a new house, and furniture for it and a servant to maintain it, he withdraws in disgust. Chremes, on the other hand, is so anxious to see the arrangements succeed that he will agree to anything, and even says that he has the cash ready. He is the very embodiment of acquiescence and the gesture aptly expresses this.[132]

The same gesture is made by another Chremes in another play: *Heauton timorumenos*. Scene 3 of its Act III finds this elderly character in the company of his slave, Syrus, and his son, Clitipho. Syrus is anxious to disembarrass himself of the company of the son since it looks as if the latter's behaviour may jeopardize his own plan for relieving the father of some of his money, but the young man resists his suggestion that he withdraw and declines a further invitation to go off in any direction he pleases. After an exchange between the two, Chremes intervenes to give his approval to the wishes of the slave with an expression of his agreement – 'recte dicit; censeo' – which he reinforces with this hand-signal.[133]

We then have, here, four examples of the gesture being associated with expressions of agreement in the text, and we also find it related to indications of approval.

Take, for instance, two of the miniatures of *Adelphoe*. The dénouement of the play begins with the fourth scene of Act V where Demea is reflecting on his past life. He concludes that he has much to learn from his brother, whose easygoing nature he has so often criticized, and he decides that he would do well to forego his own natural harshness of

---

[132] P 164r, C 85v, J&M I, nos. 747–8.

[133] *Heauton timorumenos* 588: 'He speaks aright; I agree.' P 81v, C 42v, J&M I, nos. 380–1.

disposition and adopt the more emollient ways of Micio. He quickly gives effect to this new resolution and when the servant, Syrus, appears in the next scene (V, 5), he tells him that, despite the fact that he is a slave, there is something about him that is by no means ignoble, adding further that he will be glad to do him a good turn if occasion arises (vv. 886–7). When, in the following scene (V, 6), another slave, Geta, enters, he praises him too, and also offers to do him a good turn (vv. 891–6). Geta thanks him for his kind opinion and Demea informs the audience that his affability is improving with practice:

> meditor esse adfabilis,
> et bene procedit.[134]

To each of the slaves portrayed in the separate illustrations of the two scenes,[135] he gives the gesture we have been describing. He evidently associates it with affability, but it is an affability which he interprets as the expression of approval to those in a lower station of life than himself as we see from the extravagant way in which he extols the second slave:

> Geta, hominem maxumi
> preti esse te hodie iudicaui animo meo.
> nam is mihi profectost servo' spectatus satis
> quoi dominu' curaest, ita ut tibi sensi.[136]

The same gesture is used by Thais in the miniature relating to the text of Act III, scene 2 of *Eunuchus*[137] where approval is clearly intended for, if with one hand she gives our present signal, with the other, she points to the eunuch whose handsome appearance she is praising in the script: 'ita me di ament, honestust.'[138] Her own commendation is, in fact, reinforced by another character on stage who speaks of the eunuch's accomplishments in literature, music, the arts, and athletics. Thais is here declaring her approbation of someone else, and there is another occasion towards the end of the play when she is the subject of approval herself. This is

---

[134] *Adelphoe* 896–7: 'I'm studying to be affable, and it's going well.'

[135] P 120r (where the gesture is not well understood), C 62v, J&M I, nos. 558–9; and P 121r, C 63r, J&M I, nos. 563–4.

[136] *Adelphoe* 891–4: 'Geta, today I have come to the conclusion that you are a very worthy fellow: for it's a tried and proved servant who takes care of his master's interests as I have perceived you to do.'

[137] P 47r, C 24v (where the gesture is less clear than in P), J&M I, nos. 203–4.

[138] *Eunuchus* 474: 'As the gods love me, he is good-looking.'

when, in scene 9 of Act V, Chaerea is expressing concurrence with his brother's choice of wife, who is none other than Thais herself. While displaying the gesture of approval in the accompanying illustration,[139] he observes:

nil est Thaide hac, frater, tua
digniu' quod ametur: ita nostrae omnist fautrix familiae.[140]

Her support, of course, has consisted of restoring to the family a long-lost sister, which action is depicted in the illustration to scene 6 of Act IV, where she is seen using the selfsame gesture (pl. XXI*b*)[141] as she expresses her feelings of approval for the girl whom she is presenting to her suitor (v. 748).

Recourse is also made to the same gesture when, in Act V, scene 8, during the resolution of the play, Chaerea learns that there are no further obstacles to his marrying the woman he loves. He is ecstatic with joy and declares that no man is happier than himself and that heaven has heaped all its blessings on him. He thanks Parmeno for having been the promoter of his bliss as he tells him that he is now betrothed to his beloved. Parmeno gives his warm approval – 'bene, ita me di ament, factum'[142] – confirming this with our present hand-signal.[143] It must be said that the fact that both Thraso and Gnatho follow suit will seem odd when we recall that the first had himself been a contender for the lady's hand and the second had been his agent. Nevertheless, we know from the next scene that they were both anxious to keep on good terms with the lady concerned and this may explain why they are associating themselves, outwardly at least, with this show of goodwill towards the successful suitor.

To our four instances of the gesture being called upon to indicate agreement, we can, then, add five more where it can be linked with expressions of approval. The tenth and final example of its use can only be understood in terms of an earlier stage of the plot of *Eunuchus*. It occurs in the miniature relating to Act IV, scene 5.

---

[139] P 65r, C 34r, J&M I, nos. 316–17, where it is described as Act V, scene 8, v. 1049.

[140] *Eunuchus* 1051–2: 'Nothing is more deserving of affection, brother, than your Thais here; she has been such a support for our whole family.'

[141] P 55v, C 29r, J&M I, nos. 254–5.

[142] *Eunuchus* 1037: 'As the gods love me, that's well done!'

[143] P 64v, C 33v, J&M I, nos. 310–11.

This features the young man Chremes, who on his first appearance before the audience confides to them that he is tipsy, and his unsteady gait in the Vatican portrayal certainly suggests as much. In this inebriated state, he tells the servant-girl, Pythias, that she seems lovelier than ever and she responds by referring to his own merriment. Yet, the point of the scene is not to entertain us with a little badinage but to inform us of the rift that has arisen between Thais and the soldier. It tells us that they had had a violent quarrel – 'lites factae sunt inter eos maxumae'[144] – and had parted from each other some time ago. Now, this would have been like music in Pythias' ears for – as we shall see in the course of our discussion of the gesture for apprehension – she had already, in the first scene of this Act, shown herself anxious about the relationship between her mistress and the military man and fearful that he might do her harm. It is for this reason that she gives our gesture of approval here.[145] Such is not suggested by the text, but it is certainly appropriate to the action.

A similar gesture is made by a marble figure in the Louvre, signed by the sculptor Kleomenes and thought to represent a member of Augustus' family in the role of Hermes the Orator;[146] and also by a marble representation of Apollo.[147] However, in the gesture made by these figures, the second, third and fourth fingers are bent and not extended, which suggests that it is, in fact, the oratorical gesture for approval described by Quintilian, a gesture analogous to our own but not quite the same: 'pollici proximus digitus mediumque ... unguem pollicis summo suo iungens remissis ceteris est ... adprobantibus ... decorus.'[148]

PUZZLEMENT

Although, as we have seen earlier, our last gesture would be easily comprehended today, this is far from being true of our next. If a person pointed a finger at his face, or forehead, as he addressed us, we would surely be puzzled. Our sense of perplexity would have a certain appro-

[144] *Eunuchus* 734.   [145] P 55r, C 28v, J&M I, nos. 249–50.

[146] See Bianchi Bandinelli, *Rome: the Centre of Power*, pl. 47 and pp. 47 and 400.

[147] Reinach, *Répertoire de la statuaire grecque et romaine* I, 249, pl. 486A (no. 905E).

[148] XI.iii.101 (ed. Radermacher II, 347): 'When the tip of the first finger touches the middle of the adjacent thumb-nail, the other fingers being relaxed ... we have a becoming gesture ... for those expressing approbation.'

priateness, for this, in terms of the Terence miniatures, is the signal for puzzlement itself.

It is, in fact, the first of the gestures to be illustrated in *Eunuchus* (I, 1). This opens with a problem – the one of Phaedria's that we have referred to earlier in a different context. 'Quid igitur faciam?' he asks,[149] and he soon lets us know what his difficulty is. It is whether to accept an invitation from his mistress. He is quite besotted with her, but she has shown herself so unpredictable in the past – now allowing him into her house and now shutting him out – that he does not know which way to turn. Later, after telling us that he is torn between his love and loathing of her, he refers to his perplexity again by repeating that he does not know what to do: 'nec quid agam scio.'[150] As he voices this puzzlement in the text, he is shown in the accompanying illustration[151] pointing a finger towards his face. This gesture, with slight variations – it can be one or two fingers pointing to the face or forehead – is repeatedly associated with figures who find themselves in puzzling situations. Prominent among them continues to be Phaedria.

At another stage of the action (IV, 2),[152] we find him beset with more heart-searchings about the same lady (pl. XXX*a*). She has persuaded him to go into the country for two days, although much against his will, and once there, he begins to ask himself whether his decision was a wise one:

> hem biduom hic
> manendumst soli sine illa?[153]

In a further bout of vacillation, he goes on to consider that, even though he has agreed to a separation, he need not have permitted it to be such a complete one; he might have remained closer to his beloved so that, even if he could not touch her, he might at least have had some sight of her. His puzzled musings on the subject in this scene are shattered by a problem of a more devastating kind in the next, although one still relating to the mistress he is sighing for. One of her servants, Pythias, bursts on to the scene in a state of incoherent panic which obviously takes him aback, and she continues to be inarticulate until she comes to her real point, which is that the eunuch he had earlier presented to Thais has ravished one of the women in her household. As one might

---

149 *Eunuchus* 46: 'What am I to do?'   150 *Eunuchus* 73.
151 P 36r, C 19v, J&M I, nos. 167–8.   152 P 51v, C 27r, J&M I, nos. 233–4.
153 *Eunuchus* 636–7: 'What, must I stop here for two days alone without her?'

expect, the response of Phaedria is of disbelieving bewilderment: 'qui istuc facere eunuchu' potuit?'[154] In the accompanying illustration,[155] the artist has given him the same gesture of puzzlement as in the previous scene.

If Phaedria, so much on the outside, was perplexed by the unexpected virility of a eunuch, how much more must have been someone more involved, like the father of the eunuch himself – or rather the father of the young man who was masquerading as one – when told that his son has taken the place of the real eunuch and has now been apprehended as an adulterer (V, 5). Indeed, he is so confounded that at first he can only repeat the significant words of the message being relayed to him on the subject: 'is pro illo eunucho ad Thaidem hanc deductus est', says his informant, and the old man simply echoes, 'pro eunuchon?'[156] His puzzlement is implicit in the situation and the artist shows him pointing a finger to his face (pl. XXII*a*).[157]

The introduction of a counterfeit eunuch into the play naturally gives cause for uncertainty to a number of its characters, the most unsophisticated of whom is Pythias, the servant who had broken the news of his disastrous intrusion to Phaedria. The subject of her puzzlement is the most elemental of all. Here is a man who has shattered the tranquillity of the household, who has ravished an innocent maiden in it, and whose supercilious excuse has simply been that he believed her to be one of the servants (her own class) whereas, in fact, she was a girl for whom her mistress had a special concern. Over and above all else, that same mistress has put the blame for this disaster entirely on Pythias. Her problem, then – expressed to the accompaniment of this gesture[158] – is a simple one: how to get even with the brute who has caused such havoc, or at least with the person who has introduced him into their household:

> quid, quid uenire in mentem nunc possit mihi,
> quidnam qui referam sacrilego illi gratiam
> qui hunc supposiuit nobis?[159]

---

[154] *Eunuchus* 657: 'How could a eunuch do this?'
[155] P 52v, C 27r, J&M I, nos. 238–9.
[156] *Eunuchus* 991–2: 'He was taken to Thais in place of that eunuch.' 'In place of a eunuch?'
[157] P 62v, C 32v, J&M I, nos. 292–3.
[158] P 60r, C 31v (where the gesture is not well defined), J&M I, nos. 275–6.
[159] *Eunuchus* V, 3, 910–12: 'If I could only think of something, some way of paying back the scoundrel who palmed this fellow off on us!'

Naturally, the plots of other plays provide their own problems for the characters to deal with: uncertainty about a lady's chastity in *Heauton timorumenos*, and uncertainty about how to react to an assault on it in *Hecyra*.

Act II, scene 2 of the first play finds Clinia, who has recently returned from abroad to see his loved one, now eating his heart out because she has not appeared at the agreed rendezvous. He begins to think the worst, and as he gives this gesture (pl. XXII*b*),[160] he perplexes himself with the thought that, during his absence, she may have been led astray. Were not all the circumstances, he asks himself, conducive to this – the opportunity, the place, her age, and the dominance and wickedness of her mother, who thinks only of money? Pamphilus, in the second play, has also been away on foreign soil, and we have seen that he discovers soon after his return that his wife has been made pregnant since he parted from her. His first problem is how to respond to her distraught mother's supplication that he keep her condition a secret. The second, and more weighty, one is whether to take her back or no. This clearly gives him much to puzzle about for he refers both to the bond that love and a shared life have knit between them (v. 404), and to the fact that tears come to his eyes when he thinks of her living out a lonely life by herself (vv. 405–6). As he reflects upon the apparently insoluble problem that has confronted him (III, 3), his use of our present gesture, with two fingers pointing to the face,[161] seems appropriate even though we do learn at the end of his tale what his final decision has been.

There is another long soliloquy by another unhappy character, who is also faced with a thorny problem, in Act IV, scene 4 of *Adelphoe*. Indeed, the scene actually begins with the outcry he gives about his dilemma:

> Discrucior animi:
> hocin de inprouiso mali mihi obici tantum
> ut neque quid me faciam nec quid agam certu' siem![162]

The character is Aeschinus, and his difficulty is also associated with a lady although not, as it happens, one of his own choosing. She is the mistress of his brother, whom he has been trying to help, and it is only because of

---

160 P 73v, C 38v, J&M I, nos. 349–50.   161 P 134v, C 70r, J&M I, nos. 623–4.

162 *Adelphoe* 610–11: 'What torment of the mind! To be suddenly confronted with such an unexpected calamity so that I know neither what to do with myself nor what course of action to take!'

this that he has become involved with her. At a time when his own beloved is expecting his child, his association with the other woman has unfortunately become known, and his dilemma is that he is unable to reveal the true cause of this relationship without betraying his brother. 'Nunc quid faciam?' he says in the text as he points with two fingers to his forehead in the accompanying miniature.[163]

In his illustrations of *Phormio*, the artist has given this gesture to four of its characters, all in a state of some perplexity – a son, a father, a lover and a wife.

The son is Antipho who, having married in his father's absence and without his consent, is awaiting his return in a fearful state of trepidation. He is now puzzling himself as to whether he had been wise to marry a penniless girl without his parent's knowledge. If he had made a different choice, he is reflecting, it would probably have gone hardly with him for a few days, but he would not have had to endure the daily anguish of spirit that he suffers now (I, 3, vv. 159–60).[164] His feelings of dubiousness about his past action shine clearly through.

The father is his own – Demipho – who has hoped to release Antipho from this alliance in order to free him for a more appropriate one. Demipho has paid Phormio to marry the woman concerned himself but, having parted with his money, he is seen in Act V, scene 2[165] wondering whether he was wise to deal with this kind of person. His slave Geta's apparent uncertainty about whether Phormio will indeed keep his side of the bargain – he can only say that he hopes he will do so – increases Demipho's misgivings and he anxiously asks whether there really is a doubt: 'etiamne id dubiumst?'[166] Any uncertainties that he may have are certainly not dispelled by Geta's answer that he does not know since the man may change his mind, and by now, Demipho is so puzzled by it all that he decides to send for his brother to discuss the situation with him.

The lover is Phaedria, whose problem in Act III, scene 3[167] is also to do with money – indeed, how to get access to it at all. The object of his passion is a slave-girl, a musician whom he had hoped to purchase, but the slave-dealer has told him that, unless he can raise the necessary money

---

[163] *Adelphoe* 625: 'What am I to do now?' P 113v, C 59r (where the gesture is not too clear), J&M I, nos. 524–5.

[164] P 152v, C 79r, J&M I, nos. 694–5.

[165] P 168v, C 87v (where the gesture is too low), J&M I, nos. 767–8.

[166] *Phormio* 774.   [167] P 162r, C 84r, J&M I, nos. 732–3.

by the next day, she will be sold to another client. Unfortunately for the infatuated young man, he has no money and no source from which he might find it, and in his frustration and desperation, he cries out:

> Quid faciam? unde ego nunc tam subito huic argentum inueniam miser, quoi minu' nihilost?[168]

The wife is Nausistrata who, in Act V, scene 9, sees her husband enter the room in an obvious state of distress and fear, which he refuses to explain, and, what is more, in the company of a complete stranger who is subjecting him to verbal attacks in his own home. The newcomer then becomes anxious to give her a message which her husband tries to stifle, or at least persuade her to disbelieve. Faced with this baffling situation, she has every cause for puzzlement and for the use of this gesture.[169]

It is one that Simo calls on three times in *Andria*. The first is when, in Act II, scene 4,[170] he is listening to the brief conversation between Davus and Pamphilus, and is puzzled to know what scheme they are up to. The second is when he is perplexed to find in Act III, scene 4[171] that, contrary to all his expectations, his son is now actually agreeing to his suggestion that he marry the daughter of a neighbour, despite his earlier betrothal to the girl whom he really loves. The third is when, in Act V, scene 4,[172] he is told that the same girl is not an unknown immigrant, as everyone had thought, but a freeborn citizen and, what is more, a lost daughter of that very neighbour whose other daughter he had been so keen to have as a daughter-in-law. However, all this raises conundrums. Is the man from Andros, who is providing the crucial testimony, really an honest person? What was the actual name of the person who, he claims, had originally been shipwrecked with the girl? How is it that she then had a different name from the one she claims for herself now? The doubts which have to be resolved in the course of his enquiries are puzzling ones, each one of which would be enough to attract the use of this gesture.

[168] *Phormio* 534–5: 'What am I to do? Where can a poor wretch like me get the money from so quickly when I have less than nothing?'
[169] P 174v, C 91r, J&M I, nos. 794–5.
[170] P 15r, C 9v (where the gesture is less clear than in P), J&M I, nos. 63–4.
[171] P 21r, C 12r, J&M I, nos. 103–4.   [172] P 32r, C 17v, J&M I, nos. 154–5.

LOVE

As we have seen, the chief cause of the uncertainties that arise in *Eunuchus* is the existence of two eunuchs, one real and the other counterfeit. It is a situation that has been contrived by Chaerea, whose own problem is that he has conceived a passion for a young girl to whom access is difficult and who can only be approached in some sort of disguise. It is because of this that he has borrowed the clothes of the real eunuch and masqueraded as one himself.

Soon after his first sight of the woman who has set his heart on fire, he meets Parmeno and enters into an ecstatic description of her (II, 3). He speaks of the loveliness and uniqueness of her face, the naturalness of her complexion, the firmness and plumpness of her limbs, and of the fact that he can never again consider another woman. In the course of this eulogizing, he goes on to express his passion quite unambiguously by declaring 'amo'.[173] At a later stage of the action (III, 5), when he has attained his purpose, he is even more impassioned in his outburst to Antipho. In this state of elation, he declares that he is so happy that he could face death itself before his joy is sullied by the mundanities of life, that he is in a delirium of ecstasy, that the girl herself is beyond compare, that he is inflamed with a passion for her, and again he comes to the point with an unequivocal statement that, in short, he has fallen in love:

> in hac commotu' sum . . .
> quid multa uerba? amare coepi.[174]

In each of the relevant illustrations (pl. XXIII*a* and *b*),[175] Chaerea is shown holding a slightly curved hand across the top of his head, and since both scenes are so entirely imbued with his expression of love and its related feelings, this can mean only one thing and that is love itself. It is an interpretation which is confirmed by the fact that, according to the artist, Chaerea's rival Thraso also produces the same gesture in Act V, scene 9[176] when he speaks of his love for the same lady (even though by

---

[173] *Eunuchus* 307.

[174] *Eunuchus* 567–8: 'I was stirred by her. Why waste words? I fell in love.'

[175] P 42v, C 22v (where the gesture is less clear than in P), J&M I, nos. 192–3; and P 49v, C 25v, J&M I, nos. 220–1.

[176] P 65r, C 34r, J&M I, nos. 316–17, where it is described as Act V, scene 8, v. 1049.

now he knows that he has lost her): 'quanto minu' spei 'st tanto magis amo.'[177]

FEAR, APPREHENSION

Yet, whatever the feelings of affection towards Thais that the soldier expresses here and elsewhere, the view of one of her women is that she has reason to fear him for, as she explains to the audience, she had noted how quickly he can lose his temper and also seen how prepared he has been to act against the wishes of the woman he claims to love. Dorias, therefore, opens Act IV[178] by confiding to the audience that:

> quantum ego illum uidi, non nil timeo misera,
> nequam ille hodie insanu' turbam faciat aut uim Thaidi.[179]

Later (IV, 3),[180] on hearing the dreadful news that the eunuch, the unnatural monster as she is to call him, has ravished a girl in her household, Dorias is understandably fearful again, as her cry of 'perii' demonstrates.[181] On each occasion she is represented as making a particular gesture in the illustrations which consists of throwing both forearms upwards. It has some resemblance to a specifically Christian gesture that we find in the paintings of the catacombs and in other areas of early Christian art – the *orans* position for prayer – but in our Terence illustrations it is the gesture for apprehension. The gesture was already known to Roman art in this sense, for we find it used, for example, by Diana in a sarcophagus carving of the rape of Proserpina.[182]

At one point in the Terence, the gesture is put to ironic use. When, in Act III, scene 2 of *Andria*, Simo learns that his son, Pamphilus, is to acknowledge the child of his beloved as his own, he realizes that this will thwart his own plans for marrying him to his neighbour's daughter but then decides – quite incorrectly – that this is simply part of a story being put about by Davus to frustrate his own arrangements. So he tells the slave that he should not suppose that his master is a fool, and that he

---

[177] *Eunuchus* 1053: 'The less hope there is for me, the more I love her.'
[178] P 51r, C 26v, J&M I, nos. 227–8.
[179] *Eunuchus* 615–16: 'From what I have seen of him, I'm wretchedly afraid that that madman will today cause an affray or do some violence to Thais.'
[180] P 52v, C 27r, J&M I, nos. 238–9. [181] *Eunuchus* 664: 'I'm done for!'
[182] Robert, *Einzelmythen*, pp. 466–7 (no. 377) and pl. CXXII.

should at least try to give the impression of being afraid lest his pretence be discovered: 'saltem accurate, ut metui uidear certe, si resciuerim.'[183] The fact that Davus responds by throwing up his arms in the gesture of fear[184] suggests that he is here being sardonic for he knows full well that, on this occasion at least, he is guiltless: in fact, Pamphilus' statement has been to the detriment of his real plans.

The apprehension which evokes this gesture in an earlier part of the same play (Act I, scene 5)[185] is caused by something overheard concerning the Andrian girl of the title. She is in childbed and her nurse, Mysis, is already on her way to fetch a midwife when she inadvertently learns something that gives her a fright. It is that the father, who has promised to marry her mistress that very day, has had the same day chosen for him to marry another, and she bursts out with the cry that the remark has frightened her almost to death: 'oratio haec me miseram exanimauit metu.'[186] She has need of the gesture again when faced with another anxious moment (IV, 3).[187] This is when the slave Davus, after telling her to wait for a moment in the street, disappears into a house and suddenly reappears with a tiny baby which he insists that she take from him.

The anxiety of the nurse in *Phormio* (V, 1)[188] concerns the disservice she believes she has done her charge by advising her to marry Antipho simply because of financial pressures: 'nam uereor era ne ob meum suasum indigne iniuria adficiatur.'[189] Then, as she is reflecting on this, and on her inability to trace the girl's own father who has been long absent, she is given a sudden fright by his appearance from the background where he has been skulking all the while, and makes our present gesture (pl. XXIV*a*).

It also expresses the fears of Myrrina in *Hecyra* (pl. XXIV*b*) which are not related to others but to herself (IV, 1).[190] As we have already seen, she has been concealing from the world and from her own husband the shameful fact that her daughter has been made pregnant by an unknown assailant, and now that the child has been born, she is concerned lest her

---

[183] *Andria* 494: 'At least make it seem as though I would cause fear if I were to find out.'
[184] P 18r, C 11r, J&M I, nos. 91–2.   [185] P 9v, C 7r, J&M I, nos. 42–3.
[186] *Andria* 251.   [187] P 26r, C 14v, J&M I, nos. 125–6.
[188] P 167v, C 87r, J&M I, nos. 762–3.
[189] *Phormio* 730: 'For I am afraid that, as a result of my persuasions, my mistress may be shockingly wronged.'
[190] P 138v, C 72r, J&M I, nos. 638–9.

husband should discover its presence in the house. On his entrance, however, he makes it all too clear that she has not been successful in keeping the secret, and strongly censures her for trying to do so. He then accuses her of wanting to do away with the infant and of trying to break up her daughter's marriage, and, as he gets even more angry, he forbids her to remove the baby from the house. He, of course, still thinks that his son-in-law is the father, a belief actually encouraged by Myrrina herself (v. 528), and when he is out of the room, she reflects on her own wretchedness and the dreadful situation now facing her. She has just witnessed one of his tempers, and she now asks herself what his anger will be like if he is ever informed of the real situation which, she persuades herself, will indeed happen, for if her son-in-law thinks that another man's child is being foisted on himself, he will surely reveal everything and divulge all that she has gone to such lengths to conceal (vv. 575–6).

GRIEF, SADNESS

If the concealment of the original pregnancy leads to problems between Myrrina and her husband, it gives rise to even more acute ones between the parents of her son-in-law, for neither is aware of the real situation. They have no idea that their daughter-in-law has simply left their home to conceal her condition, and her action is put down to a difference she has had with her mother-in-law, Sostrata. For this the older woman is given the blame, and such is certainly the belief of her husband during the course of much of the play. He makes this particularly clear in Act III, scene 5, where he says that she is the root of all the trouble, and as a consequence will find herself the recipient of his spleen (v. 515). Earlier, his view had been given some apparent support by a remark made by the girl's father (II, 2, vv. 267–71) which he does not fail to note (v. 271), and in the next scene (II, 3), Sostrata expresses her unhappiness in a sad soliloquy on the unfairness of a world which causes all women to be hated by their husbands because of the offences of a few:

> nam ita me di ament, quod me accusat nunc uir, sum extra noxiam.
> sed non facile est expurgatu: ita animum induxerunt socrus
> omnis esse iniquas.[191]

---

[191] *Hecyra* 276–8: 'For so help me heaven, I am innocent of what my husband now

There is a more simple reference to her state of misery in the preceding scene – 'heu me miseram'[192] – and in the accompanying picture she lays a hand to the side of her face to express her sadness (pl. XXV).[193]

Of all moods, it was grief that attracted the most varied forms of expression in classical art, and this we have enlarged on in the previous chapter.[194] 'Grief' is perhaps too grave a word to apply to the comedies of Terence, although the characters do experience the frustrations and distresses of everyday life and are quite capable of thinking at times that the world has come to an end. On such occasions, they give expression to their despondency by holding a flat or curved hand to the side of their face, as does Sostrata here, and this we have earlier shown has its parallel in a similar gesture for grief presented by a terracotta figurine of a stage character made some centuries before (pl. XIV*a*). Another possible distress-gesture in the Terence is the lifting up of the cloak to conceal the face and partly dry the eye, as represented by Aeschinus in an illustration to *Adelphoe* (IV, 5).[195] This has a classical parallel in the sculpture of a mourning young man in the Louvre,[196] the only real difference between the two portrayals being that Aeschinus is forced to use his left hand to raise his cloak since he is making a speech-gesture with his right. Despite this, the parallel is probably accidental and the action, which only occurs in this one miniature, can be very simply explained in terms of the text which tells us that the character concerned has burst into tears after hearing the dreaded news that his beloved is being sent abroad, and is unable to look his father in the face (vv. 679 and 683). Other than this, as we have said, the signal for sadness or wretchedness in our miniatures is the one displayed by Sostrata. We find it presented elsewhere by a slave sorrowing for his mistress, a youth at variance with his loved one, and a father distressed by his son.

The slave is Geta, who in *Adelphoe* (III, 2) finds that it is his duty to break to his widowed mistress, Sostrata, the melancholy news that the

---

accuses me of. But it is no easy matter to clear myself when they have made their minds up that all mothers-in-law are harsh.'

[192] *Hecyra* 271. [193] P 131v, C 68r, J&M I, nos. 603–4.

[194] See above, p. 33.

[195] C 59v, J&M I, no. 530. This is not shown in P which simply shows the left arm under the cloak, but it is taken over in F.

[196] Paris, Musée du Louvre, Ma 4. See Baratte and Metzger, *Catalogue des sarcophages en pierre d'époques romaine et paléochrétienne*, no. 17 and pl. on p. 58.

man who has promised marriage to her daughter, who is herself already in childbed by his offspring, has left her for another woman. This will be discussed further below, but in the meantime, it may be said that it is understandable that, as the bearer of such a depressing message, Geta should feel sadness himself, and that he should express this by our present gesture.[197]

The youth is Clinia who, because of a misunderstanding in *Heauton timorumenos* (II, 3), believes that the modest girl he had left behind when circumstances forced him to go abroad and whom he has now returned to see, has taken advantage of his absence. By certain means, she has succeeded in making herself so wealthy that she can now afford jewels and garments and a veritable troop of servants, and he works himself into a thoroughly depressed condition about his fears. He bemoans the fact that, whereas he has been prepared to alienate himself from his father and go into exile for her sake, she has not remained faithful to him, and he declares that no one is more wretched than he: 'nemost miserior me.'[198] It is because of this that he can give the signal of sadness (pls. XIV*b* and XXXVI*a*).[199]

But his father has cause to use this, too, when after treating the son on his return with considerable, if surreptitious, generosity and attempting to achieve a reconciliation, he learns from Menedemus of the youth's unbridled extravagance in attaching to himself a courtesan with a pronounced taste for luxury, the costs for which will threaten him with ruin (vv. 908–9). He therefore gives our present gesture for despondency in the miniature to Act V, scene 1. This is according to the Paris manuscript.[200] However, since this does not agree with the Vatican miniature, questions concerning the transmission of the illustrations arise which will necessitate a brief digression.

The Paris manuscript illustrates the scene with four figures: Menedemus (who is giving Chremes the information about his son) is shown with the gesture for speech, Chremes has the one for sadness, Clitipho the one for speech, and Syrus the one for compliance. The Vatican manuscript offers a completely different picture.[201] This simply has two figures,

[197] P 105r, C 55r (where the gesture is ill-defined), J&M I, nos. 490–1.
[198] *Heauton timorumenos* 263.   [199] P 74r, C 39r, J&M I, nos. 355–6.
[200] P 90r, J&M I, no. 426.   [201] C 47r, J&M I, no. 427.

namely Menedemus, again with the gesture for speech, and Chremes, now with the gesture for surprise. Where we might expect an illustration for scene 2, the Paris manuscript leaves a blank, but the Vatican codex gives us the picture that Paris had provided for scene 1 with the figures, other than Syrus, reidentified. Here, it is Clitipho and Chremes who have the *adlocutio* gesture while Menedemus presents the gesture for sadness, and Syrus remains with the gesture for compliance.[202]

Such an obvious discrepancy between the Paris and Vatican manuscripts has naturally elicited interest from scholars both past and present, and among them, Jones and Morey have taken the view that the Paris illustrator continued a mistake in the archetype which has been corrected by the Vatican one.[203] Grant, however, offered a different explanation.[204] He argued that there had originally been one illustration to cover both scenes 1 and 2, and that the reason for the present differences is as follows. An original scribe had encountered in his textual model a scene-heading (i.e. the display of the names of ensuing characters which normally prefaced each illustration) for scene 2, and so he left a space for an expected picture. This, however, was not forthcoming in the artistic model which the original miniaturist used, and he therefore simply left the blank as it was. In this view, the miniature in Paris correctly reflects the original, and illustrates both scenes 1 and 2. This would be appropriate in terms of the gestures used. The same hypothesis has led Grant to the belief that the Vatican artist filled the blank space he found before scene 2 with a picture, adapted to the needs of that scene (as it certainly is), but based on the miniature already in place before scene 1. This meant giving new identities to the figures other than that of Syrus, and it also meant that a new illustration had to be created to meet the needs of scene 1. This picture, as we see it now, is therefore an invention of the Vatican copyist. In the view of the present writer, there is a point in that illustration which may seem to favour Grant's hypothesis. It is the positioning of the arm in the gesture being made by Chremes. This is meant to signify surprise, but it is out of keeping with the use of the gesture of surprise elsewhere[205] where the hand is held at about chest-level (see pl. XXVII *a* and *b*), whereas here it is held aloft at the level of

---

[202] C 48r, J&M I, no. 431.   [203] J&M II, 58.

[204] Grant, *Studies in the Textual Tradition of Terence*, pp. 38–9.

[205] See below, pp. 80–4.

the ear. Grant suggests that the present illustration was modelled on that to IV, 5, but since this has a gesture for compliance which does not play a part in the miniature we are discussing, he might have been better advised to have suggested the miniature for IV, 6. However all this may be, I shall myself be following the views of Grant in this study and shall make this clear where there is need.

SUPPLICATION

After delivering his doleful message to his mistress, Geta decides, with her agreement, that the sensible way to help her in the present crisis is to approach a neighbour, Hegio, and ask for his help. This he does by beseeching Hegio with the declaration:

> in te spes omnis, Hegio, nobis sitast:
> te solum habemu', tu es patronu', tu pater:
> ille tibi moriens nos commendauit senex:
> si deseris tu periimus.[206]

In the course of this entreaty, Geta introduces another gesture into our illustrations: the one for supplication in which the slightly bent arms are held out imploringly (pl. XXVI).[207]

Chaerea has recourse to it in the illustration to Act V, scene 2 of *Eunuchus* (pls. XXIX*b* and XLVI*a*)[208] when he is supplicating Thais on two counts. First, he begs forgiveness for having ravished one of the women in her household:

> unam hanc noxiam
> amitte: si aliam admisero unquam, occidito.[209]

Further, he seeks her help in arranging a marriage between himself and the girl he has wronged:

> nunc ego te in hac re mi oro ut adiutrix sies,
> ego me tuae commendo et committo fidei,

---

[206] *Adelphoe* III, 4, 455–8: 'All our hopes, Hegio, rest on you. There is no one else, you are her protector and father. My old master entrusted us to you on his death-bed: if you forsake us we are lost.'

[207] P 109r, C 57r, J&M I, nos. 504–5.   [208] P 58v, C 30v, J&M I, nos. 269–70.

[209] *Eunuchus* 852–3: 'Forgive me for this one offence, and if I ever commit another, kill me!'

TERENTI

I Vatican City, Biblioteca Apostolica Vaticana, Vat. lat. 3868, 2r.
Frontispiece illustration with bust of Terence.

IIb Vat. lat. 3868, 2r (detail). Terence.

IIa Vatican City, Museo Vaticano, Braccio Nuovo. The emperor Philip the Arab.

IIIa Merseyside Museums, Ince Blundell Collection, no. 232. Figure of an actor (detail of a sarcophagus).

IIIb Vat. lat. 3868, 2r (detail). Figure of an actor.

IVb Vat. lat. 3868, 65r. Comic mask for *Hegyra.*

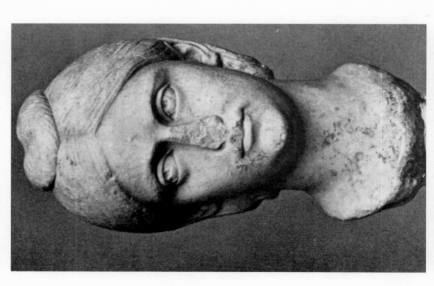

IVa Copenhagen, Ny Carlsberg Glyptotek,
Inv. no. 1493 (cat. 757). Marble head, perhaps
of the empress Salonina.

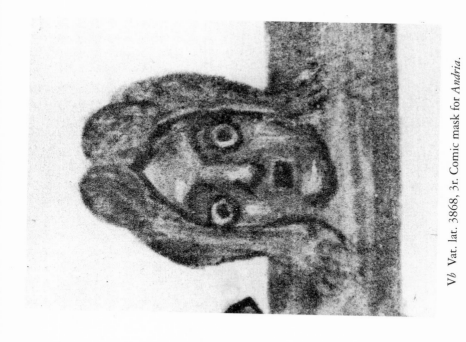

Vb Vat. lat. 3868, 3r. Comic mask for *Andria*.

Va Vienne, Musée Saint-Pierre, Mosaic of the
Victorious Athletes. Comic mask.

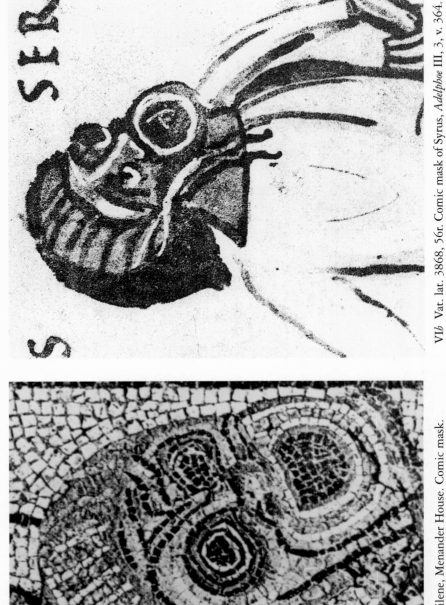

SER

S

VIb Vat. lat. 3868, 56r. Comic mask of Syrus, *Adelphoe* III, 3, v. 364.

VIa Mytilene, Menander House. Comic mask.

VII*a* El Djem, Maison des Mois, Room 3. Tragic mask.

VII*b* Vat. lat. 3868, 35r. Comic mask for *Heauton timorumenos*.

VIII*b* Vat. lat. 3868, 65r. Comic mask for *Heyra*.

VIII*a* New York, Metropolitan Museum of Art, Rogers Fund, 1910 (10.210.68). Terracotta comic mask.

IX*b* Rome, Catacomb of Priscilla, Cubiculum of the *Velatio*, back wall. Mother and child.

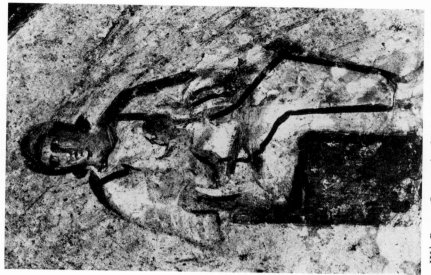

PYTHIAS ANCILLA

IX*a* Vat. lat. 3868, 30r. Pythias, *Eunuchus* V, 1.

X*b* Vat. lat. 3868, 66r. Appeal for silence (?):
Philotis, *Hecyra* I, 1.

X*a* Vat. lat. 3868, 72v.
Eavesdropping: Laches, *Hecyra* IV, 2.

XI Vat. lat. 3868, 3r. Comic mask for *Andria*, with one raised and one lowered eyebrow.

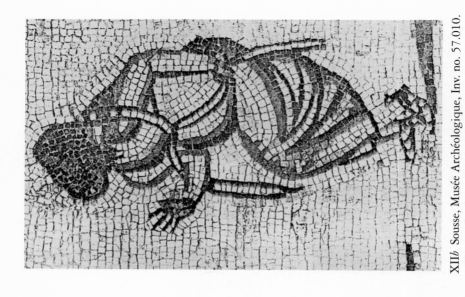

XII*b* Sousse, Musée Archéologique, Inv. no. 57.010. Figure of a slave, from a mosaic depicting a scene from comedy.

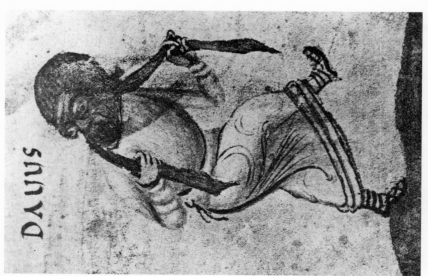

DAVVS

XII*a* Vat. lat. 3868, 18r. The slave Davus: *Andria* V, 5.

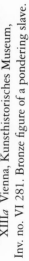

XIII*b* Paris, Bibliothèque Nationale de France,
lat. 7899, 41r. The slave Parmeno: *Eunuchus* II, 2.

XIII*a* Vienna, Kunsthistorisches Museum,
Inv. no. VI 281. Bronze figure of a pondering slave.

XIV*b* Vat. lat. 3868, 39r. The sorrowing
Clinia: *Heauton timorumenos* II, 3.

XIV*a* Athens, National Archaeological Museum,
Inv. no. 13015. Sorrowing figure.

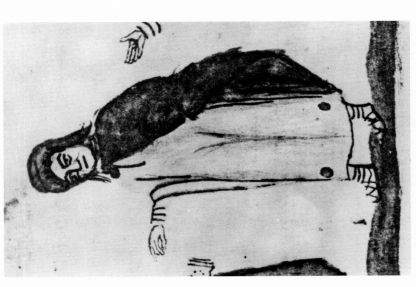

CNREMES SENEX

XV*b* Vat. lat. 3868, 42r. Insistence: Chremes,
Heauton timorumenos III, 2.

XV*a* Vat. lat. 3868, 82v. Refutation: Hegio,
Phormio II, 4.

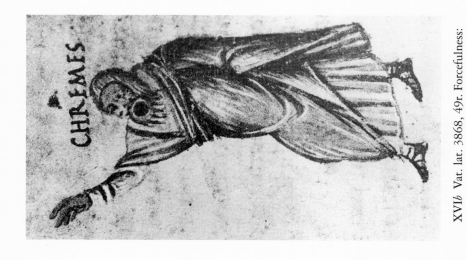

XVI*b* Vat. lat. 3868, 49r. Forcefulness:
Chremes, *Heauton timorumenos* V, 3.

XVI*a* BN lat. 7899, 99r.
Forcefulness: Demea, *Adelphoe* I, 2.

XVII*a* Vat. lat. 3868, 57r. Restraint: Demea, *Adelphoe* III, 4.

XVII*b* Vat. lat. 3868, 86v. Restraint: Demipho, *Phormio* IV, 5.

XVIII*b* Milan, Biblioteca Ambrosiana, S.P. 4 bis (formerly H 75 inf.), 11v. Belligerence: Thais, *Eunuchus* V, 1.

XVIII*a* Vat. lat. 3868, 80r. Belligerence: Demipho, *Phormio* II, 1.

XIXb Vat. lat. 3868, 54r. Compliance: Syrus, *Adelphoe* II, 3.

XIXa BN lat. 7899, 78r. Compliance: Menedemus,
Heauton timorumenos III, 1.

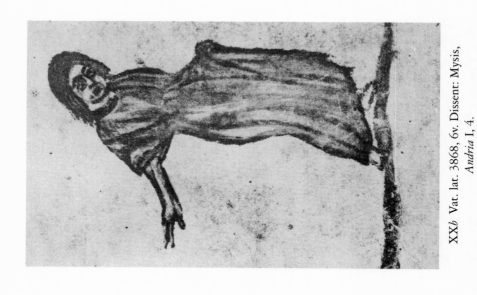

XX*b* Vat. lat. 3868, 6v. Dissent: Mysis,
Andria I, 4.

XX*a* Vat. lat. 3868, 37v. Dissent: Clitipho,
Heauton timorumenos I, 2.

XXI*b* BN lat. 7899, 55v. Approval: Thais, *Eunuchus* IV, 6.

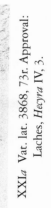

XXI*a* Vat. lat. 3868, 73r. Approval: Laches, *Hecyra* IV, 3.

XXIIa BN lat. 7899, 62v.
Puzzlement: Laches, *Eunuchus* V, 5.

XXIIb BN lat. 7899, 73v. Puzzlement:
Clinia, *Heauton timorumenos* II, 2.

XXIII*a* BN lat. 7899, 42v. Love: Chaerea,
Eunuchus II, 3.

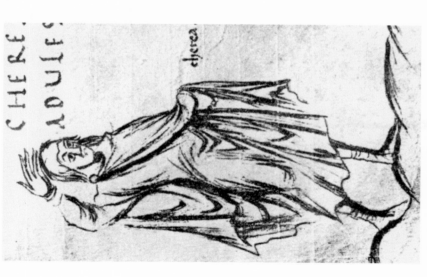

XXIII*b* BN lat. 7899, 49v. Love: Chaerea,
Eunuchus III, 5.

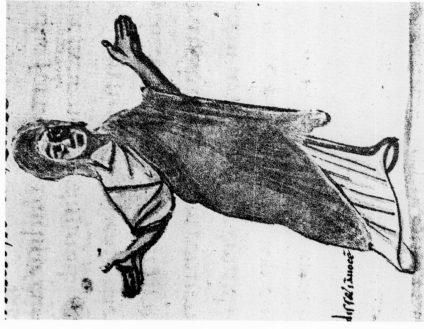

XXIV*b* Vat. lat. 3868, 72r. Fear: Myrrina, *Hecyra* IV, 1.

XXIV*a* Vat. lat. 3868, 87r. Fear: Sophrona, *Phormio* V, 1.

SOSTRATA
MULIER

XXV BN lat. 7899, 131v. Sadness: Sostrata, *Hecyra* II, 2.

XXVI BN lat. 7899, 109r. Supplication: Geta, *Adelphoe* III, 4.

XXVIIb BN lat. 7899, 53v. Surprise: Dorias, *Eunuchus* III, 3.

XXVIIa Vat. lat. 3868, 55r. Surprise: Canthara, *Adelphoe* III, 1.

XXVIII Vat. lat. 3868, 56r. Pondering: Demea, *Adelphoe* III, 3.

XXIX*a* Vat. lat. 3868, 85v. *Phormio* IV, 3.

XXIX*b* BN lat. 7899, 58v. *Eunuchus* V, 2.

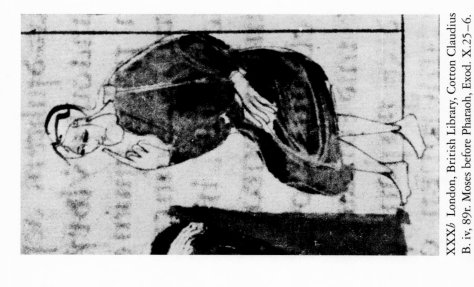

XXX*b* London, British Library, Cotton Claudius
B. iv, 89r. Moses before Pharaoh, Exod. X.25–6.

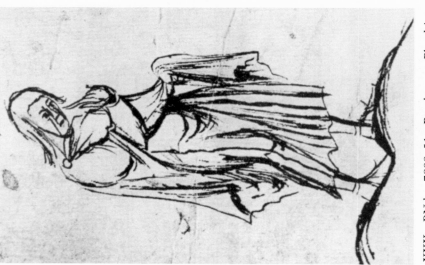

XXX*a* BN lat. 7899, 51v. Puzzlement: Phaedria,
Eunuchus IV, 2.

XXXI Claudius B. iv, 121v. Aaron, from the scene depicting the Lord
telling Moses of the rod that will blossom, Numbers XVII.1–5.

XXXIIb Claudius B. iv, 54r. More uncertainty over what should be the fate of Joseph, Gen. XXXVII.25–8.

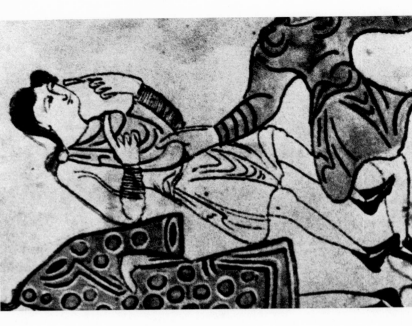

XXXIIa Claudius B. iv, 54r. Two of the sons of Jacob puzzling over what should be the fate of Joseph, Gen. XXXVII.18–22.

XXXIII*b* Claudius B. iv, 49r. A servant receiving Jacob's instructions, Gen. XXXII.13–19.

XXXIII*a* Claudius B. iv, 56r. One of the men of Timnath responds to Judah's friend Hirah, Gen. XXXVIII.20–1.

XXXIV BL Royal 6. B. VIII, 1v. Opening initial of the Prologue of
Isidore's *De fide catholica*.

XXXV*b* BL Cotton Tiberius C. vi, 11v.
Peter at the Washing of the Feet.

XXXV*a* Rouen, Bibliothèque Municipale,
Y. 6 (274), 32v. Joseph at the Nativity.

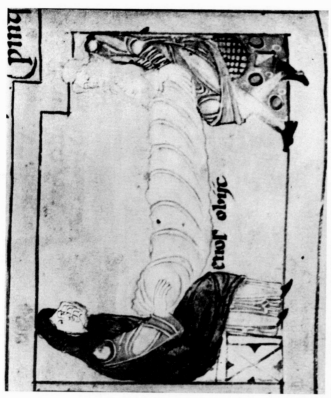

XXXVIb Claudius B. iv, 10v. The widow of Enos grieves over her husband's dead body, Gen. V.11.

XXXVIa BN lat. 7899, 74r. Grief: Clinia, *Heauton timorumenos* III, 3.

XXXVII Claudius B. iv, 139v. The children of Israel mourn the death of Moses, Deut. XXXIV.8.

XXXVIII*a* Claudius B. iv, 42v. Isaac laments his mistaken
blessing of Jacob in place of Esau, Gen. XXVII.30–5.

XXXVIII*b* Claudius B. iv, 54v. Jacob grieves at the sight of Joseph's
coat of many colours, Gen. XXXVII.32–4.

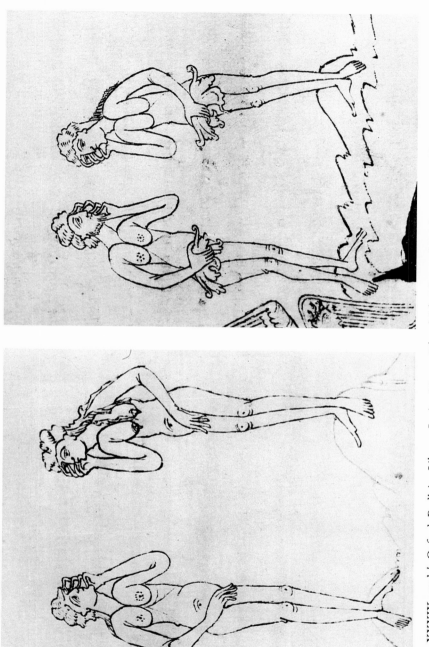

XXXIX*a* and *b* Oxford, Bodleian Library, Junius 11, pp. 34 and 36. Adam and Eve lament their fall, cf. *Genesis* 765–80.

XL*a* BL Harley 603, 67v. The Israelites lament their sins, cf. Ps. CXXX.3.

XL*b* Harley 603, 70r. The Israelites weep by the rivers of Babylon,
Ps. CXXXVI.1.

XLI*a* Harley 603, 72v. The psalmist laments his plight,
Ps. CXLI.

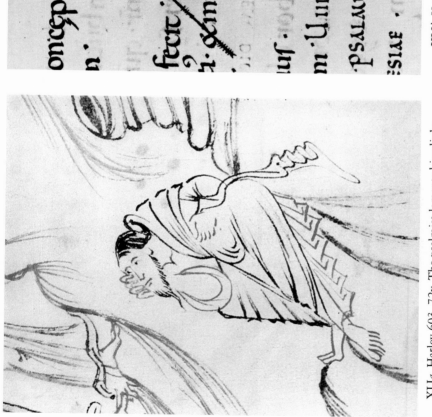

XLI*b* Vatican, Reg. lat. 12, 25r. The personified
Unrighteousness laments, cf. Ps. VII.11–17.

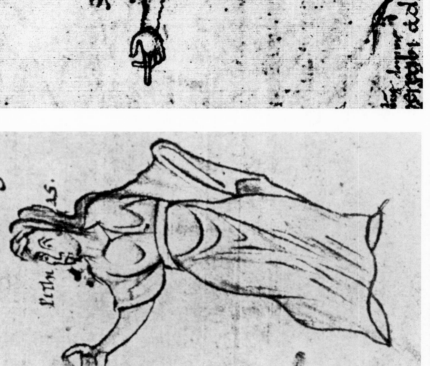

XLIIa Milan, Biblioteca Ambrosiana, S.P. 4 bis, 8v.
Approval/acquiescence: Pythias, *Eunuchus* IV, 5.

XLIIb S.P. 4 bis, 36v. Approval/acquiescence: Syrus,
Heauton timorumenos III, 3. v. 593.

XLIII BL Arundel 155, 133r. St Benedict approves the humility of the
Christ Church brethren.

XLIV*a* Arundel 155, 10r. St Benedict flanked by two monks.

XLIV*b* Arundel 155, 9v. St Pachomius receives the Easter tables
from an angel.

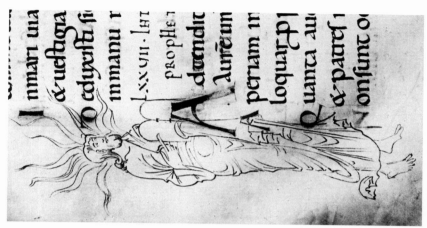

XLVb Reg. lat. 12, 83v. Moses displays the tablets of the law, cf. Ps. LXXVI.21.

XLVa Vatican, Reg. lat. 12, 88r. God the Father approves the psalmist's appeal, cf. Ps. LXXVIII.8–12.

XLVI*a* BN lat. 7899, 58v. Supplication:
Chaerea, *Eunuchus* V, 2.

XLVI*b* Claudius B. iv, 69r. The Egyptians appeal to Joseph for corn,
Gen. XLVII.15.

XLVII*a* Claudius B. iv, 35r. Abraham
before Abimelech, Gen. XX.9–16.

XLVII*b* Claudius B. iv, 24r. Abraham receives the Lord's promise,
Gen. XIII.14–17.

XLVIII*b* Oxford, Bodleian Library, Junius 11, p. 87. Abraham before the Lord, cf. *Genesis* 1806–8.

XLVIII*a* Claudius B. iv, 51v. Jacob receives the Lord's command to build an altar at Beth-el, Gen. XXXV.1.

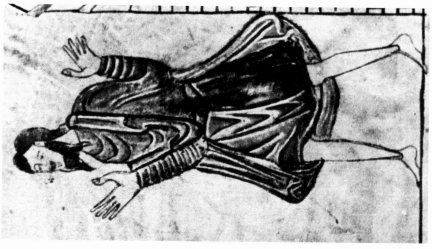

XLIX*a* Vat. lat. 3868, 26v. Fear: Dorias, *Eunuchus* IV, 1.

XLIX*b* Claudius B. iv, 33r. Lot beholds his wife being turned into a pillar of salt, Gen. XIX.26.

L Claudius B. iv, 31v. Lot receives the angels who bear news of the impending destruction of Sodom, Gen. XIX.1–3, 12–13.

LI*a* Claudius B. iv, 28r. Hagar in the wilderness, Gen. XVI.7.

LI*b* Claudius B. iv, 35v. Abraham before
the Lord, Gen. XXI.12–13.

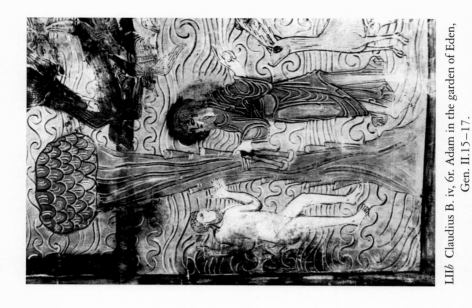

LII*b* Claudius B. iv, 6r. Adam in the garden of Eden, Gen. II.15–17.

LII*a* Claudius B. iv, 26v. Abraham before the Lord, Gen. XV.1.

LIIIa Claudius B. iv, 55v. The messenger before Tamar, Gen. XXXVIII.13.

LIIIb BL Cotton Tiberius C. vi, 12r. The arrest of Christ.

LIV*b* Claudius B. iv, 141r. Rahab and the two Israelite spies, Josh. II.1.

LIV*a* BN lat. 7899, 107r. Pondering: Demea, *Adelphoe* III, 3, v. 364.

LV Claudius B. iv, 28r. Abraham and Hagar at the time of Ishmael's birth,
Gen. XVI.15–16.

te mihi patronam capio, Thai'. te obsecro:
emoriar si non hanc uxorem duxero.[210]

The slave Parmeno may also be giving this gesture in the illustration to Act V, scene 5[211] of the same play as he entreats his master not to blame him for the unpalatable news he has to convey: namely that one of his two sons has bought a eunuch to give to a courtesan and that the other has fallen in love with a music-girl and has been imprisoned as an adulterer. Parmeno's gesture is not entirely clear but it is allied with the forward running action with which our present gesture tends to be associated.

Another slave in another play – *Andria* (IV, 1) – also finds a use for the gesture. The fact that the youth Pamphilus is in love with one woman, whereas his father wants him to marry another, who has captured the affections of Pamphilus' friend, leads of course to complications and plottings, and the slave Davus takes a leading part in these. When, therefore, things go wrong, Pamphilus can find it convenient to turn to the servant and put the blame for his difficulties on him. In the event, the latter readily accepts responsibility, and to the accompaniment of this gesture,[212] he solicits Pamphilus for his forgiveness. He says that it is his part as a servant to work day and night and even risk his neck for his master, but that if anything unforeseen does happen, it is the part of the master to forgive: 'tuomst, siquid praeter spem euenit, mi ignoscere.'[213]

This same gesture is made familiar to us by its appearance in classical painting and metalwork, and also in sculpture, where barbarians, for example, are represented beseeching their Roman conquerors for mercy with similar uplifted hands.[214] A late example of the gesture in Roman art is to be found on a coin of *c.* 306 representing the entry of Constantius Chlorus into London[215] where the action of the personified city is described by one distinguished scholar as that of welcoming the

---

[210] *Eunuchus* 885–8: 'I beg you now to assist me in this matter. I commend and commit myself to your trust, I take you as my advocate, Thais. I implore you: I will die if I do not have her as my wife.'

[211] P 62v, C 32v, J&M I, nos. 292–3.   [212] P 23r, C 13r, J&M I, nos. 116–17.

[213] *Andria* 678.

[214] One example is that of the barbarians making their supplication to Marcus Aurelius which is represented on a relief panel in the Musei Capitolini, Rome, reproduced by Becatti, *The Art of Ancient Greece and Rome*, fig. 324.

[215] Now in the Rheinisches Landesmuseum, Trier, and illustrated in Bianchi Bandinelli, *Rome: the Late Empire*, pl. 187.

emperor[216] although, in fact, she is supplicating: supplicating presumably for the protection of Rome to continue.

SURPRISE, AMAZEMENT

When her daughter is in childbed, Sostrata's own gesture of supplication to the nurse, Canthara, is to reinforce the entreaty she is making for information on how the latter thinks the labour will go (*Adelphoe* III, 1, v. 288).[217] However, Canthara's response is not a particularly sympathetic one and she replies: 'iam nunc times, quasi numquam adfueris, numquam tute pepereris?'[218] She is clearly surprised at the premature nature of Sostrata's anxiety, and the gesture she gives to express this (pl. XXVII*a*) is one in which the arm is half-folded, and the hand held out from the side as if to receive something. Although the artist can sometimes show the arm more closely folded and the hand itself either flatter or more raised, this is his gesture for surprise, as other illustrations confirm.

One is for the next scene (III, 2)[219] where the artist again gives this hand-signal to Canthara, who is confronted with surprises enough. She has been pointing out the more comforting aspects of the situation to Sostrata – the father is an excellent young man who comes from a good home and is so solicitous about the mother-to-be that he visits her every day – but she is quickly to discover how mistaken she has been. She learns that the young man whom she has just been praising, the one whom her own mistress has spoken of as being the life and hope of them all (v. 331), and who has sworn that he could not survive a single day without her love, has forsaken her for another woman. Even without this, the manic appearance of Geta who imparts this formidable information would have been an occasion for amazement, and so too, the advice he gives to his widowed mistress that she refer her misfortune to someone else. At this point, Canthara finds it impossible to contain her astonishment and cries out:

---

[216] *Ibid.*, p. 432.   [217] P 104v, C 55r, J&M I, nos. 485–6.

[218] *Adelphoe* 290: 'Are you fearful already, as though you have never been present at a childbirth or had a baby yourself?'

[219] P 105r, C 55r, J&M I, nos. 490–1.

au au, mi homo, sanun es?
an hoc proferendum tibi uidetur esse?[220]

Demea, one of the brothers in the same play, also gives this gesture to express amazement. This is when, in searching for his brother (IV, 2),[221] he encounters the latter's slave, Syrus, who is actually helping Demea's son to avoid his father but who does not mind causing embarrassment to the father in the process. Unfortunately, the stories he manufactures are not always consistent or credible, and Demea learns to his incredulity that his son is not in the country as Syrus had only recently asserted (III, 3), that the route which will take him to his brother will involve him walking right through a blind alley, and furthermore, that the said brother is not in the kind of area where he might be expected to be. The old man is not slow in pointing out these discrepancies (vv. 560, 578 and 584), but, nevertheless, the greatest surprise that the slave has in store for him is of a more pleasant kind. It is that the reputation of his son, which Demea had always seen as a glowing testimonial to his own theories of parenthood but which had been tarnished by his involvement in an unfortunate escapade, can now be redeemed by the new story that Syrus wishes him to believe: which is that he (the slave) was actually the person mainly responsible for the offence, and furthermore that Demea's son has already punished him for it with a sound thrashing.

In fact, this very slave had only just presented the gesture to the son as an expression of his incredulity at the other's inability to think up for himself a pretext for claiming to be away when his father returns (IV, 1).[222] And he joins with another slave in making use of the gesture towards the end of the play (V, 7).[223] Here they have every reason to do so for they are witnessing a change in Demea's customary conduct that is quite amazing. He has described himself in Act V, scene 4 as being boorish, harsh, disconsolate, niggardly, grim and stingy – 'ego ille agresti' saeuo' tristi' parcu' truculentus tenax'[224] – and these are the characteristics by which everyone has known him. What the servants do not know, however, is that he has privately resolved to change his approach to life and emulate the easygoing ways of his brother. They themselves have

---

[220] *Adelphoe* 336–7: 'Gracious, man, are you in your right senses? Do you think this ought to be disclosed?'

[221] P 111v, C 58r, J&M I, nos. 514–15.   [222] P 110v, C 58r, J&M I, nos. 509–10.

[223] P 121v, C 63r, J&M I, nos. 568–9.   [224] *Adelphoe* 866.

been the subjects of his first experiment as we saw in our discussion of the gesture for agreement, but what is happening now is something far more dramatic. After so much embittered criticism of his brother and his brother's son, Demea has so far reversed his attitudes to them that he has decided to share his home not only with them but with the son's wife and mother-in-law as well, and the slaves are now being instructed to put all this to practical effect by taking down the wall that separates the two houses. There is no talk of their incredulity in the text, but it is made very clear by their use of the signal for it in the illustration. Indeed, the brother himself has recourse to the gesture in the very last scene of the play (V, 9) when personally commenting on Demea's surprising change of heart – 'quid istuc? quae res tam repente mores mutauit tuos?'[225] – which has prompted him to press for the slave Syrus and his wife to be given their freedom, and in the same picture the slave also signals surprise at the unexpected, if hoped for, turn of events.[226]

The fact that the illustration which the Vatican manuscript supplies for *Heauton timorumenos* Act V, scene 1[227] may be an invention of the copyist has been discussed above but, nevertheless, Chremes' gesture of surprise in it is in keeping with the text. He has convinced himself that his proposal of a marriage between his daughter and the son of Menedemus will not be accepted except as a trick for getting money that will, in fact, find its way into the hands of the courtesan Bacchis, and he has told Menedemus as much. He is therefore nonplussed to find that this is not so, and that there has been no talk of any money being given in the exchanges between Menedemus and his son about the subject. His dialogue with his neighbour runs as follows:

Chr. hoc priu' scire expeto,
quid perdideris. nam ubi desponsam nuntiasti filio,
continuo iniecisse uerba tibi Dromonem scilicet,
sponsae uestem aurum atque ancillas opus esse: argentum ut dares.
Men. non. *Chr.* quid? non? *Men.* non inquam. *Chr.* neque ipse gnatu'? *Men.* nil
prorsum, Chreme.
magis unum etiam instare ut hodie conficiantur nuptiae.

---

225 *Adelphoe* 984: 'What is this? What has happened to cause you to change your ways so suddenly?'
226 P 123v, C 64r, J&M I, nos. 577–8.
227 C 47r, J&M I, no. 427, where Chremes' hand is raised higher than is usual in this gesture. For a discussion of this, see above, pp. 77–8.

Chr. mira narras. quid Syru' meu'? ne is quidem quicquam? *Men.* nihil.
Chr. quam ob rem, nescio.[228]

In *Eunuchus*, the gesture is associated with attitudes to another and younger Chremes. This is the youth who, when asked in the most pressing and cordial of terms by Thais to visit her again, refuses in such a brusque and ill-mannered way that her maid, Dorias, is clearly astonished (III, 3).[229] Her action alone (pl. XXVII*b*) expresses her feelings for, in fact, she has nothing at all to say in the scene. Nor has she much to say in Act IV, scene 4, where she simply responds to a question, but where, once again, she can let her gesture speak for her.[230] In the previous scene, she has been told the dreadful news that their domestic eunuch has ravished one of the women of the household, tearing her clothes and pulling her hair in the process, and leaving her in a condition of complete distress. On hearing this, she decides to add barbs of her own to the infamy poured on the eunuch's absent head by Pythias, and she declares that he is a monster of a man (v. 655), guilty of an unheard-of wickedness (v. 664). Suddenly – quite literally within seconds of her latter comment – the monster himself is dragged forth from his place of concealment and set before her: an occasion for surprise, to say the least, to any young woman in her position.

However, he is not the real culprit, and Pythias becomes more vocal than her mistress would like when, in Act V, scene 2, the actual miscreant, Chaerea, makes an appearance with a view to making his peace with Thais, and Pythias sees the amiability with which her mistress treats him despite the fact that he compounds his offence by his effrontery. He begins by dismissing the whole incident as a trifle, 'paullum quiddam',[231] at which the servant explodes:

[228] *Heauton timorumenos* 890–7: *Chremes*: 'First I want to know how much it cost you. For when you told your son of the betrothal, I expect Dromo dropped a word about the clothes, jewels, and maids that the bride would need, and asked for money.' *Menedemus*: 'No.' *Chremes*: 'What? No?' *Menedemus*: 'No, I say.' *Chremes*: 'And your son neither?' *Menedemus*: 'Not a word, Chremes. He pressed me only that the marriage be celebrated today.' *Chremes*: 'I'm amazed by what you say. And how about my man, Syrus? Did he have nothing to say?' *Menedemus*: 'Nothing.' *Chremes*: 'I can't think why.'

[229] P 48r (where Dorias is mislabelled as Pythias), C 25r, J&M I, nos. 209–10.

[230] P 53v, C 27v, J&M I, nos. 244–5.   [231] *Eunuchus* 856.

> eho 'paullum', inpudens?
> an paullum hoc esse tibi uidetur, uirginem
> uitiare ciuem?[232]

Chaerea then goes on to the mocking comment that he had thought the girl he had ravished was a fellow-slave, 'conseruam'.[233] Pythias is clearly surprised – a sentiment she expresses by a version of our present gesture (pl. XXIX*b*)[234] – at the ready way in which Thais accedes to his overtures, accepting his offer of friendship, and going so far as to say that she will help him marry the woman he has wronged. Finally, when Thais even invites the man into the house which he has desecrated, Pythias cannot contain her astonishment and bursts out:

> hunc tu in aedis cogitas
> recipere posthac?[235]

In *Phormio* (I, 4),[236] Phaedria finds this gesture a useful indicator of the surprise he feels at the distracted state of Geta when he is first seen, and at the unexpected news Geta brings that Phaedria's uncle has suddenly made an appearance. In *Hecyra* (IV, 2),[237] Pamphilus uses it to buttress his sense of surprise at the information being given to him by his mother. This is that she has decided to retire to the country in order to remove the real impediment to the happiness of his marriage, which she has been told is herself. In fact, as we have already seen, Pamphilus knows full well that his marital problems have nothing to do with his mother and everything to do with his wife. In the following scene, it is the turn of Sostrata to make use of this gesture when a statement of her husband's gives her occasion for surprise, as we shall see a little later.[238]

---

[232] *Eunuchus* 856–8: 'A trifle, you rogue! Do you think it a trifle to violate a freeborn maiden?'

[233] *Eunuchus* 858.

[234] P 58v (where the palm of the hand is not extended enough), C 30v, J&M I, nos. 269–70.

[235] *Eunuchus* 897–8: 'Are you really thinking of receiving this man into your home after what has happened?'

[236] P 153r, C 79v, J&M I, nos. 699–700.   [237] P 140r, C 72v, J&M I, nos. 643–4.

[238] See below, p. 94.

PONDERING, REFLECTION

The next gesture – that for depth of thought or pondering – we have already considered in the section concerned with the burlesquing of slaves but, apart from its satirical use there, it is, in our miniatures, more conventionally allowed to members of the upper class, or more correctly, to two of them. The first is Demea, who, by this posture, registers the fact that he is deliberating on two occasions in two consecutive illustrations (*Adelphoe* III, 3, vv. 1 and 364; pls. XXVIII and LIV*a*).[239]

In both instances, the subject of his musings is one that we know was never far from his thoughts. It is his son who, as we have already seen, he considers to be an exemplar of the correctness of his own views on parenthood with their emphasis on discipline and control, in contrast to his brother's son who illustrates the reverse, his unruliness being the unfortunate result of an overindulgent upbringing. For a while, the course of events, as reported to him, seems to uphold his views, but there comes a time when he is dashed by news that seems to confound them. This is when he is told that the two sons have joined together in an affray, and as he stands alone on the stage in the first picture, his reflections must certainly be on the wretchedness of a world which can allow the good to be led astray by the bad, and which is the subject of his soliloquy in the adjacent text (vv. 355–64). In the second miniature, he is joined by Syrus who, in his crafty way, pitches to his master exactly the kind of story that he would most like to hear (vv. 392–6 and 404–9). As a result of a soft upbringing by a foolish father, he claims, the other boy has certainly behaved outrageously, but his own son, benefiting from a stricter and more admirable training, has been behaving immaculately and has even gone to the length of upbraiding the other youth for bringing disgrace on his family. From having been given news which overturns his ingrained concepts, Demea is now offered information which confirms them, all of which clearly needs his careful consideration. This, no doubt, is what this second use of the gesture (pl. LIV*a*) is intended to convey although there is no overt indication of his pensiveness in the text.

The second upper-class character is Simo who has been anxious for his son, Pamphilus, to marry the daughter of his neighbour Chremes, only to find the latter calling off the arrangements when he learns of Pamphilus'

[239] P 106v, C 56r, J&M I, nos. 495–6; and P 107r, C 56r, J&M I, nos. 500–1.

entanglement with another woman whom he would prefer as his wife. As Simo declares at the end of Act I, scene 1 of *Andria*, he is concerned about the suppport that the artful slave, Davus, will give to Pamphilus in the battle of wits that will follow between father and son. The opening of the next scene shows Simo making this gesture[240] as he reflects on what Davus, who does not realize he is being overheard, is unguardedly saying on the subject.

THE RELATIONSHIP OF THE GESTURES IN THE MINIATURES TO THE STAGE

This is the eighteenth gesture that we have discussed, and we have found that the gestures used by the artist signify simple pointing and speech (the *adlocutio*), but also, more significantly, eavesdropping, refuting, insistence, forcefulness, restraint, belligerence, compliance, dissent, agreement, perplexity, love, apprehension, sadness, supplication, surprise and pondering.[241] These gestures could not have been borrowed from the orators since only three of them – those for refuting, for insistence and for forcefulness – are also found in rhetoric, and the first occurs only once in the Terence.[242] Nor could they have come from the received vocabulary of artists, for the number of parallels there are also quite insignificant.[243] Indeed, if we look at the gestures of Greek art – which would, of course, have been accessible to our third-century miniaturist – and at those of Roman art, we shall see how little use he made of any of them.

We have already observed that he ignored the textual description of the shaking of hands to denote friendship in Act III, scene 1 of *Heauton timorumenos*,[244] yet this was well known in classical art to connote friendship and good feeling as Sittl,[245] Neumann[246] and Brilliant have demonstrated. Brilliant, in particular, has shown how familiar it was in the Roman world, being used on sepulchral

---

[240] P 7r, C 6r, J&M I, nos. 24–5.

[241] I do not claim these to be entirely exhaustive although they are nearly so. There are one or two other gestures for which I have found insufficient evidence to justify my putting forward conclusions.

[242] See above, pp. 24, 35–6 and 40–4.   [243] See above, pp. 31–3, 65, 75 and 79–80.

[244] P 78r, C 41r, J&M I, nos. 368–9. See above, p. 51.

[245] *Die Gebärden der Griechen und Römer*, p. 27.

[246] *Gesten und Gebärden in der griechischen Kunst*, pp. 49 and 54.

monuments to symbolize the amity between husband and wife,[247] and on coins (which would of course have had a wide circulation) to advertise the supposed friendship between Roman rulers – between Titus and Domitian[248] and between the members of the Second Triumvirate[249] – as well as between Caesar and the Roman citizens,[250] and between other emperors and their soldiers. The emperor Nerva (96–98), we learn, 'repeatedly struck an extensive coinage bearing the hortatory legend, "Concordia Exercituum", and the symbolic motif of clasped right hands'.[251] We may enlarge on this evidence for the clasped hands being a visual cliché for friendship, or comradeship, in the Roman world by pointing out that they appeared by themselves in a series of coins struck by Pupienus and Balbinus in the mid-third century,[252] the very time when we have claimed the model for the Vatican manuscript was being made. Again, we have already noted[253] the fact that the textual statement that Chremes patted a slave on the head to indicate approval in Act IV, scene 5 of *Heauton timorumenos* was not reflected in the related picture,[254] yet this action, too, seems to have had an earlier classical precedent.[255]

Apart from avoiding artistic gestures that could have been useful to him, the artist has replaced others he must have known by quite different hand-signals.

An example of this is the gesture of surprise. In Roman art it consisted of raising the hand, or hands, with the palm turned outwards as if to ward something off. This we see in contemporary carvings. They are two third-century AD sarcophagi in the Louvre, one of which shows Dionysus unexpectedly coming across the sleeping Ariadne,[256] while the other represents the response to the disclosure of Achilles, who has been concealing himself as a woman in the court of Lycomedes, as the male hero he really is.[257] According to Sittl and Neumann, other ways of indicating surprise in earlier classical art had been to raise the arms or

---

[247] Brilliant, *Gesture and Rank in Roman Art*, pp. 45–6.   [248] *Ibid.*, p. 92.

[249] *Ibid.*, p. 44.   [250] *Ibid.*   [251] *Ibid.*, p. 105.

[252] Kent, *Roman Coins*, p. 309 (figs. 443–4).   [253] See above, p. 57.

[254] P 86v, C 45v, J&M I, nos. 406–7. See lines 761–2.

[255] Neumann, *Gesten und Gebärden in der griechischen Kunst*, p. 74.

[256] Paris, Musée du Louvre, Ma 1346. See Baratte and Metzger, *Catalogue des sarcophages en pierre d'époques romaine et paléochrétienne*, no. 67 and pl. on p. 139.

[257] Ma 2120. See *ibid.*, no. 165 and pl. on p. 253.

touch the mouth.[258] Yet, in our miniatures, as we have earlier seen,[259] a quite different gesture was used: namely folding the arm and laying out the hand, palm upwards, as if to receive something. Again, for the placing of the finger on the lips, which artists before him had used as a call for silence,[260] our own has substituted the little finger being directed upwards,[261] a gesture which, according to Aristophanes, had much earlier signified contempt.[262] Then, for the action of advancing the hand towards the face or grasping the beard, which had suggested perplexity in earlier art,[263] we now have a finger pointing to the face or forehead,[264] a gesture which, like most of the others in our miniatures, finds no parallel in the art of Greece or of Rome.

In all this, it is perhaps of some relevance to point out that Sittl, in his study of gestures in Greek and Roman art, remarked on the importance of the illustrated manuscripts of Terence in providing information on dramatic gestures,[265] and even went so far as to give a list of the manuscripts concerned. But he made no attempt to analyse the gestures themselves, presumably because he realized that they belonged to a different genre from those used by artists. And this would have been a correct surmise. If our investigations show anything, it is that our repertory of gestures was peculiar to the stage. It must also have been the Terentian stage as we shall see if we look at these gestures in context and see how smoothly they all fit into the dramatic action, and respond neatly to each other.

Our analytical procedure has been to take each gesture in turn, describe every occasion on which it appears, and show that it retains the same meaning whatever its context. Although this course of action has meant examining each gesture in isolation, they do, in fact, all participate in a general flow. So, as we have already seen, Sostrata's gesture of supplication to the nurse in Act III, scene 1 of *Adelphoe* leads to the rejoinder of the gesture of surprise at her request by the latter,[266] the gesture of

---

[258] Sittl, *Die Gebärden der Griechen und Römer*, pp. 13 and 271; Neumann, *Gesten und Gebärden in der griechischen Kunst*, p. 97.

[259] See above, pp. 80–4.

[260] Sittl, *Die Gebärden der Griechen und Römer*, pp. 54 and 213.

[261] See above, pp. 23–4.   [262] Sittl, *Die Gebärden der Griechen und Römer*, p. 97.

[263] Neumann, *Gesten und Gebärden in der griechischen Kunst*, pp. 109–12.

[264] See above, pp. 65–70.   [265] Sittl, *Die Gebärden der Griechen und Römer*, p. 203.

[266] P 104v, C 55r, J&M I, nos. 485–6.

forcefulness presented by Demea in the same play (I, 2) calls forth a calming-down gesture on the part of Micio,[267] and the belligerent gesture of Thais in the illustration to Act V, scene 1 of *Eunuchus* evokes the mollifying gesture of compliance from her servant.[268] We could take any single picture from the cycle of 144 illustrations and demonstrate that the gestures in it respond not only to the dramatic action but to each other, and we can give two examples of this, the first using the Vatican, the second, the Paris recension.

Our first example is the illustration for Act IV, scene 3 of *Phormio* (pl. XXIX*a*).[269] This scene, we may recall, begins with the young man Antipho seeing his father and uncle approach and, knowing that he himself will be the subject of their exchanges, expressing an anxiety to know what his uncle will say. It is clear from his later asides to the audience that he has concealed his presence from them with a view to overhearing their exchanges, and on the left he is depicted giving the signal for eavesdropping. The slave Geta comes forward to address the elderly couple and, as we have also seen earlier, to be as emollient and agreeable as possible as he tries to persuade them to pay more and more money to Phormio for the services he has promised. The gesture he gives as he does this is, therefore, understandably the conciliatory one of compliance. Demipho also indicates compliance since he supports the early part of the bargaining; however, as the suggested price rises, he drops out and leaves the parleying to Chremes, who is personally prepared to acquiesce at almost any price, and his gesture is therefore one of agreement.

Our second example is the picture to Act V, scene 2 of *Eunuchus* (pl. XXIX*b*)[270] in which Chaerea has arrived to win over Thais in a double sense: both to beg her forgiveness for what he has done within her household and to ask her help in his attempts to marry the woman he has so wronged. His arms are therefore held out in supplication, and in response Thais holds up a restraining hand to stay his entreaties, since she has already decided to forgive him. In the background, Pythias signals the surprise she feels that her mistress can be so genial under the circumstances, a surprise that finds full vocal expression in the text.

---

[267] P 99r (where Micio's gesture is too high), C 52r, J&M I, nos. 460–1.

[268] P 57v, C 30r, J&M I, nos. 264–5.   [269] P 164r, C 85v, J&M I, nos. 747–8.

[270] P 58v, C 30v, J&M I, nos. 269–70.

Now it is hardly likely that the artist could have correctly deployed and coordinated the eighteen gestures we have discussed among the 381 figures he portrays unless he knew in advance both what each meant and the exact context in which each should appear. It is manifest from this alone that he had an intimate knowledge of Terentian productions.

One suggestion that has been made is that the artist owed his knowledge of the stage to what he had seen of the theatre in earlier artistic representations of it,[271] and the interest in such depictions in Roman art is clear enough. They are seen in houses at Pompeii and in the Villa Vavano at Stabiae as well as in the mosaics of Mytilene which we have earlier referred to. Moreover, large parts of Pompeii, Herculaneum and Stabiae still remain unexcavated. However, these known works share certain similarities which lead one to suppose that they may be drawing on a given, somewhat static, repertory and, where their gestures are concerned, I have only found a single one amongst them that duplicates anything in Terence. (This is apart from the universal gestures for pointing and for speech.) A hypothesis put forward by Grant was that the artist may not have witnesssed a production of Terence 'but had conceived the illustrations in light of other stage productions which he had seen'.[272] However, the extensive number of gestures used by the artist and the dexterity and appositeness with which he applies each to so many differing situations hardly suggest that he borrowed them from elsewhere and newly applied them here.

Grant was here trying to reconcile the opinions of Leo and of Jachmann which were very much opposed. Jachmann understandably rejected the concept of the first scholar that 'the painter followed the performances scene by scene with pencil in hand',[273] but then proceeded to the opposite extreme and affirmed that the illustrator had never seen a Terence comedy on the stage,[274] and that his illustrations – if we may make his comments

---

[271] Cf. Leo, 'Die Ueberlieferungsgeschichte der terenzischen Komödien', pp. 341–2.

[272] Grant, *Studies in the Textual Tradition of Terence*, p. 20.

[273] Jachmann, *Die Geschichte des Terenztextes*, pp. 10–11, quoting Leo: 'Der Maler hat die Aufführungen Szene für Szene mit dem Stift in der Hand verfolgt' (see F. Leo, review of E. Bethe, ed., *Terentius. Codex Ambrosianus H. 75 inf.*, p. 996).

[274] Jachmann, *Die Geschichte des Terenztextes*, p. 44: 'er sieht ihn [the dramatic content of the play] lediglich als Buchtext, gleichsam durch einen papierenen Schleier, den eine gewisse Editionstechnik zweifelhaften Wertes darüber gebreitet hatte. Auf der Bühne hat er wohl nie eine terenzische Komödie gesehen.' See also p. 16, where Jachmann says that this domination of the text has led the illustrator to serious errors.

a little more succinct – were purely literary ones based only on a reading of the text. Jachmann's more detailed views will be considered in an appendix to this chapter, but here we may say that, although any illustrator of plays would presumably have read them, this scholar's concept seems to have been that ours then simply sat down and produced his 144 pictures out of his own head. If this were so, he would have needed to examine the texts very meticulously for every indication of what might be happening on the stage. Yet there is little indication that he did this in any really exhaustive way.

We have earlier seen that in Act III, scene 5 of *Eunuchus*, Chaerea gives Antipho an account of his foolhardy escapade to see the woman who has suddenly obsessed his thoughts. After insinuating himself into her household, he says that his impersonation of the real eunuch was so successful that he was even asked to fan her as she lay asleep after her bath, and he continues:

> ego limis specto
> sic per flabellum clanculum.[275]

On speaking this line, the actor would obviously have needed to hold up his hand and peer around it in imitation of the action he is describing, but there is no suggestion of this in the illustration.[276]

Nor of the action of Laches in Act III, scene 5 of *Hecyra*. At this point of the play, he is striving to reunite his estranged son and daugher-in-law, and in the process, is claiming that she will be returned to her marital home by her father, Phidippus. He turns to the latter to confirm this, but the other's testy retort, 'noli fodere',[277] tells us that, on the stage, Laches was using his elbow as well as his tongue. This has not been taken up by the miniaturist.[278] Another example of a familiarity, undesired by the character involved and totally ignored by the artist, is that of Davus towards Mysis in Act IV, scene 4 of *Andria*. This is known to the reader by her angry response to his presumptuousness when they are left alone on the stage – 'ne me attingas, sceleste'[279] – but there is no sign of it in the attached miniature.[280]

---

[275] *Eunuchus* 601–2: 'I secretly took a sideways look at her from behind the fan, like this.'
[276] P 49v, C 25v, J&M I, nos. 220–1.   [277] *Hecyra* 467: 'Don't dig me in the ribs.'
[278] P 137r, C 71r, J&M I, nos. 633–4.
[279] *Andria* 789–90: 'Don't touch me, you rogue!'
[280] P 26v, C 15r, J&M I, nos. 132–3.

When, in *Eunuchus* (II, 3), Chaerea first decides to take seriously the half-jesting remark of Parmeno's that he should dress as a eunuch and is urging the slave to come inside with him and get things ready, we know from Parmeno's indignant response – 'quo trudi'? perculeris iam tu me. tibi equidem dico, mane'[281] – that he was actually being pushed through the door by Chaerea to hasten him on his way, but the artist has made no attempt to represent this in the miniature.[282] And the same is true of a similar action elsewhere. This is in the third scene of Act III of *Heauton timorumenos*, where Syrus is so anxious to have a private word with Chremes that he persuades him to send his son out of earshot. On the stage, we know that the parental pressure was reinforced by physical persuasion on the part of Syrus since the son curses him for pushing him away – 'di te eradicent, Syre, qui me hinc extrudis!'[283] – but again, there is no evidence of this in the illustration.[284]

Our artist even disregards pointing gestures, necessary for the action and made unmistakable in the script.

An example of this is in Act IV, scene 7 of *Adelphoe*, where the remark of Micio to Demea that the lady shall be moved from that house to this – 'illinc huc transferetur uirgo'[285] – would make no sense on the stage unless the speaker were first to indicate Sostrata's house and then his own, yet no account is taken of this in the related miniature.[286] Another example is in the illustration to Act III, scene 3 of *Heauton timorumenos* to which we have just referred,[287] in which Syrus tells Clitipho 'abi sane istac, istorsum, quouis':[288] the artist does not show the directions being indicated, any more than he follows the text in showing the same slave finally pushing Clitipho away.

Now, there is one simple reason why the artist should have omitted actions that may seem important to us today. It is that his interest lay elsewhere.

He could quite easily have presented Chaerea holding up a hand, with fingers spread out to form a make-believe fan around which he could peer

---

281 *Eunuchus* 379: 'Where are you shoving me? You'll knock me over in a moment. Stop, I tell you!'

282 P 42v, C 22v, J&M I, nos. 192–3.

283 *Heauton timorumenos* 589: 'The gods destroy you, Syrus, for shoving me off from here!'

284 P 81v, C 42v, J&M I, nos. 380–1.   285 *Adelphoe* 731.

286 P 116v, C 60v, J&M I, nos. 539–40.   287 P 81v, C 42v, J&M I, nos. 380–1.

288 *Heauton timorumenos* 588: 'Go that way, over there, anywhere!'

in accordance with the textual description, but this was not his concern. It was rather to show the mood of Chaerea, which here is the one appropriate for a lovelorn youth, and his right hand is therefore used to give the gesture for love. The same miniaturist could, without difficulty, have presented Chremes patting his slave on the head to express his feelings as the script demands, but he preferred to call on one of the dramatic gestures of the stage and to show him raising his two fingers in the approved gesture for compliance. And he gave the same gesture to Menedemus to indicate the latter's new attitude to Chremes, although he could have demonstrated it just as simply by literally following the text and showing him offering his hand in friendship, a gesture which we have already seen was familiar to the Roman world. But apparently, this was not part of the visual vocabulary of the classical stage. The latter was a vocabulary of moods.

Nevertheless, it cannot be too strongly emphasized that the mood presented is not necessarily the one indicated by the text. It can be one suggested by the logic of events on stage which may even contradict, and can certainly be independent of, any suggestion in the script. In other words, it represents how actors might respond to a situation on stage rather than how an artist might choose to illustrate what he had just read. Indeed, there is one instance where he had nothing to read for, as we have already pointed out, he gives a dramatic gesture to Dorias in the third scene of Act III of *Eunuchus*[289] although she has nothing to say in the text. The gesture itself is appropriate enough to the action – it is one of surprise at the discourtesy of the young Chremes.

A particularly good example of the artist overriding the text can be seen in the illustration to Act III, scene 2 of *Adelphoe*.[290] There, as we have seen earlier, it was the task of the slave Geta to inform his widowed mistress of the distressing fact that the man who had promised marriage to her daughter, now in childbed with his offspring, has left her for another woman. As he imparts his message, Geta makes the gesture of sadness, indicating thereby that he too feels the depressing nature of the news. However, there is nothing about this in the text, where only the widow is represented in a state of grief, being asked by Geta to cease her tears: 'era, lacrumas mitte'.[291] Geta's mood is presented by Terence not as

---

[289] P 48r, C 25r, J&M I, nos. 209–10; and see above, p. 83.
[290] P 105r, C 55r, J&M I, nos. 490–1. [291] *Adelphoe* 335.

one of despondency, but as one of outrage at the young man and all those linked to him:

uix sum compos animi, ita ardeo iracundia.
nil est quod malim quam illam totam familiam dari mi obuiam,
ut ego iram hanc in eos euomam omnem, dum aegritudo haec est recens.
satis mihi id habeam supplici dum illos ulciscar modo.
seni animam primum exstinguerem ipsi qui illud produxit scelus;
tum autem Syrum inpulsorem, uah, quibus illum lacerarem modis!
sublimem medium primum arriperem et capite in terra statuerem,
ut cerebro dispergat uiam;
adulescenti ipsi eriperem oculos, post haec praecipitem darem;
ceteros — ruerem agerem raperem tunderem et prosternerem.[292]

These are not the words of a person filled with sadness but of one consumed by wrath. However, sadness would have been entirely appropriate to the situation as it was played out on the stage.

Again, there is no reference in the text to the surprise which Sostrata expresses by the appropriate gesture in the illustration to Act IV, scene 3 of *Hecyra*,[293] although such surprise is endemic to the action. After all, she must have been astonished to learn from the first words of her husband that he had just been eavesdropping on the whole of her conversation with her son. His immediate acquiescence to her views must have come as no less of a surprise after she had learned from his earlier diatribes that he thought that she was a disgrace to them both, that she had turned their friends into their enemies, that she was at the root of the differences with their daughter-in-law; in short, that she was a shameless trouble-maker (II, 1).

There are other examples of the artist bypassing the text and simply using his gestures to illustrate the mood of the action, and this we have

---

[292] *Adelphoe* 310–19: 'I'm so ablaze with anger that I am almost out my mind. There is nothing I would like better than to have the whole family in front of me so that I could discharge my fury on them while my blood is up. It would meet my entreaty if I could wreak vengeance on them now. First I would throttle the life out of the old man who brought up the scoundrel. Then, as for Syrus, who put him up to it, how I would mangle him! I would seize him by the waist and dash his head to the ground so that his brains were scattered over the street. As for the young man, I would tear out his eyes and knock him down. The rest of them I would pitch into and knock them, hit them, hammer them, trample on them.'

[293] P 140v, C 73r, J&M I, nos. 648–9; and see above, p. 84.

already indicated in our descriptions of the gestures concerned. They include the amazement of two slaves at the order of their master to take down the wall between the two houses in *Adelphoe* (V, 7)[294] which is comprehensible in terms of the action, but is not suggested by anything spoken; the way that Pamphilus softens the uncompromising words to his father that Terence has put in his mouth in *Hecyra* (IV, 4);[295] and the fact that in *Eunuchus* (IV, 5), Pythias gives a gesture for approval[296] which does not relate to the immediate text but to sentiments carried through from three scenes before.

It would seem, then, that the artist was not simply following the text in any servile or academic fashion, but was aware of how actors actually reacted on the stage.

Those who would have it otherwise point to the fact that the miniaturist usually presents his characters in the order in which they speak, which is also normally the order in which they are named in the scene-headings before each scene. However, this will seem less curious if we bear in mind three considerations. The first is that these are schematic representations which make no more pretence at being naturalistic than did the actual productions on the Roman stage. The second is that these comedies of Terence are concerned with word-play and not with dramatic action, so that the speaking-parts and their order take on a degree of importance. The third is the almost ritualistic nature of Roman acting. As Beare writes:

When we reflect on the fact that all the actors wore masks and that a very large part of their lines was not spoken but declaimed to the accompaniment of the flute-player, we realize that the Roman style of acting must have differed widely from the naturalistic, conversational style of our day. Our actors talk to each other; the Roman actors declaimed to the audience. They stood, where possible, well to the front of the stage; they faced the audience ... they aimed above all things at making their words carry even to the farthest seats ... of the large, open-air theatre.[297]

Our own view rests on the points we have already made: that neither the artist's gesture for eavesdropping nor his use of the double mask could

294 P 121v, C 63r, J&M I, nos. 568–9; and see above, pp. 81–2.
295 P 141r, C 73v, J&M I, nos. 653–4; and see above, p. 58.
296 P 55r, C 28v, J&M I, nos. 249–50; and see above, p. 65.
297 Beare, *The Roman Stage*, pp. 182–3.

95

have derived from anywhere except the stage; that he maintains theatrical traditions not only in the more conventional masks but in the distinction made between classes and in the characteristics given to slaves; that he allocates to the actors their appropriate costumes and accoutrements; that he is not tied in any slavish way to the text; that eighteen of his gestures are authentic to the stage and most of them are unknown elsewhere; and that his ability to distribute them among 381 figures with such conviction and aptness to the dramatic situation indicates a professional knowledge of actual productions. Altogether, these must make a compelling case for the belief that the artist had a close knowledge of actual productions of the plays of Terence.

APPENDIX TO CHAPTER 3

The views of Jachmann

Jachmann was, of course, a distinguished textual critic and his views on the illustrations of Terence[298] have been very influential. We should therefore give some consideration to them here. They were conditioned to a limited extent by his feeling that the supposed date of the pictures could not be reconciled with the supposed date of the final productions of the Terence comedies in Rome.[299]

It is an axiom among textual critics that some texts have become contaminated during the course of transmission but, in his minute examination of every detail of each of our 144 pictures, Jachmann does not concede that some disparities of detail might be due to a like artistic contamination or to a change of circumstances for the miniaturist although, as it happens, the illustration[300] which Jachmann cites as a particularly good example of the artist's servility to the text[301] and as a

---

[298] Jachmann, *Die Geschichte des Terenztextes*, ch. 1.

[299] See his comments on pp. 11, 26 and 44.

[300] This is the one pertaining to *Adelphoe* III, 3, v. 364 (J&M I, nos. 500–1) and relates chiefly to the positioning of Dromo and Syrus in relation to the inside or outside of the house.

[301] Jachmann, *Die Geschichte des Terenztextes*, p. 16: 'zeigt sich der Maler weniger von festen Prinzipien bestimmt als davon was er aus dem Text jeweils herausliest. Das sieht man besonders deutlich in dem Bilde zu Ad. III 3ᵃ.'

classic example of his lack of experience of the stage[302] has been shown by Grant to owe its apparent lack of consistency to the fact that the artist was responding to a slightly different reading in another version of the text.[303]

Jachmann presses the point we have already alluded to that the characters of the miniaturist appear in a similar order to those named in the scene-headings and are to a large extent restricted to them, but he exaggerates considerably when he remarks on the servility of the artist to such scene-headings[304] and has himself to admit as much on one occasion.[305] Two of the vital examples that he offers[306] (they quite exceptionally show the same character duplicated in two scenes) have been shown since his day to be due to an earlier change in the stage-divisions of the text.[307] Other proffered examples, such as the failure of the artist to show Dorias remaining on stage for a scene in which she has nothing to say[308] – which incidentally allows Phaedria space to speak his sad thoughts to himself (*Eunuchus* IV, 2) – can hardly be said to carry much weight.

Two other examples he gives are claimed not only to support his theory

---

[302] *Ibid.*, p. 18: 'Die Illustration . . . bildet einen klassischen Beweis dafür dass ihm jede lebendige Bühnenanschauung fehlt; sie zeigt deutlich wie er die Bilder aus dem Papier zieht.'

[303] Grant, *Studies in the Textual Tradition of Terence*, pp. 25–6.

[304] Jachmann, *Die Geschichte des Terenztextes*, p. 20: 'dass die Bilder von den Szenentiteln abhängen, nicht umgekehrt'; and p. 22: 'in welchem Maße der Maler hinsichtlich der zu zeichnenden Figuren von den Szenenköpfen abhängig ist, lässt sich noch in mehreren anderen Fällen nachweisen.'

[305] *Ibid.*, p. 23: 'Damit soll nun nicht gesagt sein dass er sich ausschliesslich an die Szenentitel gehalten hätte', and he proceeds to give his own examples of such exceptions which pertain chiefly to very minor characters.

[306] *Hecyra* III, 4 and V, 4 (J&M I, nos. 628–9 and 673–4). As others have observed, the duplication of a character to suggest continuous movement is known to late classical art, as in the Vatican Virgil (Vatican, Vat. lat. 3225, in the miniature numbered 11 by de Wit, *Die Miniaturen des Vergilius Vaticanus*; for a description, see *ibid.*, pp. 43–5) and in the Ambrosian Iliad (Milan, Biblioteca Ambrosiana, F 205 inf., 14v; see Calderini, Ceriani and Mai, *Ilias Ambrosiana*, pl. XV and the description on pp. LIII–LIV). However, the explanation offered by Grant (see following note) makes this something of an irrelevance.

[307] Grant, *Studies in the Textual Tradition of Terence*, pp. 45–6.

[308] Jachmann, *Die Geschichte des Terenztextes*, pp. 22–3 (J&M I, nos. 233–4).

of the dominating influence of the scene-headings[309] but also to offer evidence of the artist's inability to handle non-speaking parts just because of his ignorance of actual stage-productions.[310] Yet, if we examine them briefly, we shall see that they are consonant with the dramatic action.

One relates to Act IV, scene 2 of *Phormio*[311] where the elderly Demipho and Chremes are indeed absent from the related picture although they would have been present on the stage. However, if we look at the context of the action as a whole, we shall see that there could be good reason for the omission. In the previous scene, the old gentlemen had been immersed in a particularly private conversation, and scene 2 begins with the entry of the slave Geta, who confides to the audience the progress of the plans of Phormio and himself to extort money from them in a brief monologue of only fifteen lines. Now it is vital to the unravelling of the action of the play that the explosive secret that Chremes has been discussing with Demipho (his bigamous harbouring of a second wife by whom he has had a daughter) should not be known to others at this point of the play. The same is true of Geta's plot to disembarrass the old men of some of their money. Neither side must hear, or overhear, the other and Geta makes clear in the next scene (v. 609) that he has, in fact, been concealing himself from the others. During an actual production of scene 2, the old men would no doubt retire to the back of the stage and the artist's decision to focus entirely on Geta would have its dramatic logic.

The other example given by Jachmann also relates to a brief scene (*Adelphoe* II, 3).[312] It presents a comparable situation to the one we have just quoted in the sense that a character comes on stage and is able to confide his innermost thoughts to the audience only because he believes he is alone. The character is Ctesipho, who praises his brother in over-ecstatic terms. Later, the slave Syrus emerges from the wings or the background. But Jachmann complains that the slave-dealer Sannio, who has no speaking part in this scene although he has not made an exit from

---

309 *Ibid.*, p. 20. He concludes after his comments 'dass die Bilder von den Szenentiteln abhängen, nicht umgekehrt'.

310 *Ibid.*, p. 19: 'Die Behandlung der stummen Personen ist überhaupt ein besonders wertvolles Kriterium für die Methode des Malers ... muss es sich hier zeigen ob er eine wirkliche Anschauung von den Bühnenvorgängen besitzt.' He goes on to say that our artist does very badly here.

311 *Ibid.*, pp. 19–20 (J&M I, nos. 742–3).   312 *Ibid.*, p. 19 (J&M I, nos. 475–6).

the last, is not depicted by the artist.[313] However, we know that he has been given a really brutal thrashing by Aeschinus, the brother who is being extolled (vv. 196–9), and it is not likely that he would be anxious to make himself prominent on the stage as Ctesipho expresses his adulation. Indeed, he is clearly in concealment at the beginning of the next scene when Aeschinus himself comes storming in. For the minia-turist simply to ignore his presence in his depiction of scene 3 was by no means unreasonable. One problem in Jachmann's analysis, however, is that he supposes that artists should have no discretion.

Other than these remarks, Jachmann claims that the artist makes many mistakes as a result of his misunderstanding of how the comedies would be enacted on the stage.[314] Since he gives only one example to support this generalization, we ought to give it brief consideration.

It occurs in the picture to *Eunuchus* IV, 4[315] where the real eunuch, Dorus, has been located by the blustering Phaedria who sets him before the two servants, Pythias and Dorias. Faced with an angry question why he is not in his proper attire, the eunuch explains the true facts of the matter which are that he has been forced to change garments with Chaerea who, as we have seen, was anxious to take his place. Now Jachmann argues that the fact that he is not in Chaerea's garb indicates that the artist had not seen the play where he would have observed that this frightened figure had been forced to take over the youth's attire in exchange for his own. However, the Swiss scholar cannot have it both ways. He wants us to believe that the artist had never seen a production of the play but was relying on a reading of the text; yet it is exactly in the text that the exchange is emphasized. Immediately on the appearance of the eunuch, Phaedria asks him why he has changed his attire (v. 671), and in verses 682–3 he adverts to it again. Then in verse 707, he asks the eunuch to repeat his story that he has exchanged clothes with Chaerea which he does in the next verse.

Jachmann gives us here his only example of the errors of the artist caused by his ignorance of the stage. But it is Jachmann himself who is in error. In fact, the artist *has* shown the eunuch in 'civilian' attire having

[313] *Ibid.*
[314] *Ibid.*, p. 25: 'Geht man weiter ins Einzelne, so wird man noch viele Irrtümer, die auf Verkennung des Bühnenvorgangs beruhen, finden.'
[315] J&M I, nos. 244–5. The identities of the eunuch and Phaedria have been wrongly exchanged in both C and P.

discarded the 'uniform' which eunuchs were apparently required to wear at the time. This was a colourful striped one which is briefly referred to in this very episode (v. 683) and which we see being worn by Chaerea in the illustrations to *Eunuchus* (III, 2, 4 and 5 and V, 2)[316] when he is masquerading as a eunuch. Associated with this was a Phrygian hat and it is true that the eunuch does wear this in the picture. But for a good reason. We are told that he was a worn-out and withered old man (v. 688) so that, on stage, he would presumably have been shown simply with an old man's mask indistinguishable from any other old person. The hat, however, would be sufficient to alert the spectators to the fact that, although in Chaerea's dress, underneath it all he is really the eunuch.

In all this, we are not claiming that the miniaturist made no mistakes and that Jachmann could not identify a few of them correctly. What we are saying is that they are so few and so minor that they do not bear the weight of his own thesis. Artists have their lapses and he himself remarks on the monumental task that this one had set himself in illustrating six plays. He concedes that his pictures have an antique feel and show an awareness of how actors move on the stage,[317] and despite the apparent strength of his convictions, comments at one point that 'whether the artist had ever seen one or another of the Terence comedies on the stage cannot, on the evidence of the pictures alone, be denied or affirmed'.[318] In my view it can be affirmed.

---

[316] J&M I, nos. 204, 216, 221 and 270.

[317] Jachmann, *Die Geschichte des Terenztextes*, p. 26.

[318] *Ibid.*, p. 27: 'Ob der Maler jemals eine oder die andere terenzische Komödie auf der Bühne gesehen hatte, lässt sich auf Grund der Bilder allein weder behaupten noch verneinen'.

4

Anglo-Saxon gestures

Quintilian wrote about gestures with the enthusiasm with which a highly knowledgeable and articulate composer might write about music:

manus uero, sine quibus trunca esset actio ac debilis, uix dici potest quot motus habeant, cum paene ipsam uerborum copiam persequantur. nam ceterae partes loquentem adiuuant, hae, propest ut dicam, ipsae locuntur. his poscimus, pollicemur, uocamus, dimittimus, minamur, supplicamus, abominamur, timemus, interrogamus, negamus, gaudium, tristitiam, dubitationem, confessionem, paenitentiam, modum, copiam, numerum, tempus ostendimus. non eaedem concitant, inhibent, supplicant, probant, admirantur, uerecundantur? ... ut in tanta per omnes gentes nationesque linguae diuersitate hic mihi omnium hominum communis sermo uideatur.[1]

This is great rhetoric by a great orator, although his belief in the universality of gestures is hardly borne out by the facts. The language of the hands *does* vary from group to group, and indeed from period to period – the seventeenth-century survey of gestures which I have referred to earlier illustrates one hundred and twenty gestures, only one or two of which duplicate the considerable number described by Quintilian. On the

---

[1] *Institutio oratoria* XI.iii.85–7 (ed. Radermacher II, 343–4). Translated in Watson, *Quintilian's Institutes of Oratory* II, 364:

As to the hands, without the aid of which all delivery would be deficient and weak, it can scarcely be told of what a variety of motions they are susceptible, since they almost equal in expression the powers of language itself; for other parts of the body assist the speaker, but these, I may almost say, speak themselves. With our hands we ask, promise, call persons to us and send them away, threaten, supplicate, intimate dislike or fear; with our hands we signify joy, grief, doubt, acknowledgment, penitence, and indicate measure, quantity, number, and time. Have not our hands the power of inciting, of restraining, of beseeching, of testifying approbation, admiration, and shame? ... So that amidst the great diversity of tongues pervading all nations and people, the language of the hands appears to be a language common to all men.

other hand, six centuries before Bulwer's conspectus was published in England, miniatures produced in the same country would seem to offer some support for Quintilian's contention. And they do so in a rather surprising way, for they represent the adoption by Benedictine monks of some of the very gestures that, according to the arguments put forward in the last two chapters, had been used in performances of Terence on the Roman stage. The purity of the Latin of this playwright's works goes some way to explain why they have survived through the ages, but their plots are hardly so pure, and one can understand why a tenth-century German nun, Hrotswitha, should try (however unsuccessfully) to write plays in the Terentian style that would be more wholesome from the monastic point of view. Hrotswitha's concern was the degree to which Benedictine monks made use of the texts of Terence, but in an interlude that encompassed the eleventh century, Anglo-Saxon monks were also prepared to make use of the Terentian gestures as well.

PUZZLEMENT OR PERPLEXITY

We have earlier pointed out that, although the method of indicating puzzlement in classical art was to show the character concerned moving his hand towards his face or grasping his beard, that chosen by the Terence artist was quite different and, as far as we can tell, was unique to the classical stage.[2] This was to point one or two fingers to the forehead or face. Now it is of interest to see that this was the gesture also employed by Anglo-Saxon artists to indicate puzzlement or perplexity. So, the gesture that was used, for example, by Phaedria in *Eunuchus* (pl. XXX*a*) when he was so confused by the behaviour of his mistress, Thais, that he actually says that he does not know what to do,[3] reappears in England in the unexpected context of biblical illustrations. It is especially found in a manuscript of the first six books of the bible, which is now BL Cotton Claudius B. iv.[4] M. R. James has shown that it was in the library of St Augustine's, Canterbury, between 1491 and 1497,[5] and the Kentish characteristics of mid-twelfth-century notes in it indicate that it was in

---

[2] See above, p. 88.   [3] See above, p. 66.

[4] Facsimile in Dodwell and Clemoes, *The Old English Illustrated Hexateuch*.

[5] James, *Ancient Libraries*, p. lxxxiv. It is no. 95 of the St Augustine's catalogue made between those dates (cf. *ibid.*, p. 201, and, on the date of the catalogue, p. lviii).

the south-east in that period,[6] so that a Canterbury origin seems at least probable. We can further accept the date assigned to it by Wormald, which is the second quarter of the eleventh century.[7]

This Hexateuch has attracted much academic attention because it translates the Vulgate into the vernacular and, although the translation is not unique to this volume, it represents 'the only attempt to render the text of the Old Testament into English prose on any scale before the Wycliffite bible in the fourteenth century'.[8] However, the illustrations have their own interest. They are, in fact, so frequent and cover such large areas of the pages that they give the volume the appearance of being a picture-book as much as anything else. They take the reader from the creation of the angels, which theologians associated with the creation of light,[9] and the later fall of Lucifer and his angels to the burial of Joshua (Josh. XXIV.30), and although some of the miniatures are unfinished, this has brought some advantages for the art historian. We do not need to dwell on these here, but we might remark that the pictures include one on fol. 89r which shows Moses with Pharaoh. The prophet is pointing a finger to his own face (pl. XXX*b*), and if we ask why this should be, we shall find the answer in the text. There we learn that the negotiations of Moses with Pharaoh are being held up by a problem. The Egyptian ruler has said that the Israelites may leave his country but may not take their animals with them, and this leaves Moses in a quandary. How, without their beasts, he asks, can they perform their ritual sacrifices and continue their traditional forms of service to God (Exod. X.25–6)? He is faced with a dilemma to which there is no immediate answer, and the Terentian gesture he uses is a visual statement of this. We find the same gesture again in the upper register of another unfinished picture, this one on fol. 121v. The context is the account in the Book of Numbers (XVII.1–5) of God telling Moses to have a rod designated for each of the tribes of Israel and to have the rod of the tribe of Levi inscribed with Aaron's name; the Lord then goes on to say that the twelve rods are to be laid up in the tabernacle where one of them will be made to blossom as a warning to those who are murmuring against the prophet. Aaron is portrayed giving

[6] Clemoes in Dodwell and Clemoes, *The Old English Illustrated Hexateuch*, p. 15.
[7] Wormald, *English Drawings*, p. 67.
[8] Clemoes in Dodwell and Clemoes, *The Old English Illustrated Hexateuch*, p. 42.
[9] See Dodwell, *ibid.*, p. 17.

the gesture of puzzlement (pl. XXXI) as he listens to this surprising message from on high in which he is referred to by name.

This indicator of perplexity finds a further place in the extended depiction of the disposal of Joseph on fol. 54r (Gen. XXXVII.17–28). Here it is used by two brothers to indicate their puzzlement as they conspire together on the left (pl. XXXII*a*). Their problem is how to get rid of Joseph. Should they kill him outright, they are asking in the text, or – as Reuben has suggested – leave him to languish in a pit so that his blood will not be on their hands? The latter course of action is taken, but they soon find themselves perplexed by another difficulty, which is whether to leave him where he is, or to sell him to the passing Ishmaelites. It is a predicament that is again signalled in the illustrations by one of the brothers pointing to his forehead (pl. XXXII*b*).

Another problem in another part of the same book of the Old Testament is on a vastly lower level, but it is a problem all the same (Gen. XXXVIII.20–1). In recognition of Tamar's sexual compliance, Judah has promised to send her a kid and, in the meantime, to allow her to retain his ring, bracelet and staff as a pledge. Judah tries to redeem his promise, but when the friend bearing his promised gift arrives at his destination, he finds that 'the men of that place' have no knowledge of a woman answering the description given him, and the illustration on fol. 56r shows one of them pointing to his face to indicate his perplexity (pl. XXXIII*a*).

The gesture is put to more subtle use in the depiction of another part of the Genesis story (XXXII.13–19), although it is still in the context of a presentation, this one made by Jacob to his brother Esau. The Old English text follows the Vulgate closely and reads:

He asyndrode ða lac of þam ðe he hæfde Esauwe hys breðer, twahund gata 7 twentig buccena, 7 twahund ewena 7 twentig rammena, þrittig gefolra olfendmyrena mid heora coltum, 7 feowertig cuna, 7 twentig fearra, 7 twentig asmyrena mid hyra tyn coltum. 7 he asende hys þeowas 7 ælc ðæra heorda onsundrum beforan him, 7 cwæð to him: Gyf ge gemitton Esau minne broðor 7 he eow axige hwæs ge synd, oððe hwyder ge wyllon, oððe hwa þa ðing age, þe ge mid farað, þonne cweðe ge þæt hit synd Iacobes, 7 he hi sent hys hlaforde Esauwe to lace.[10]

---

[10] Crawford, *Heptateuch*, p. 165: 'From what he had, he separated off a gift for Esau, his brother: two hundred goats and twenty he-goats, and two hundred ewes and twenty

The related picture on fol. 49r shows the servant who is receiving the orders making the gesture we are discussing (pl. XXXIII*b*). This will convey not only any puzzlement he may feel about his allotted task, but also, by transference, the perplexity of Esau himself. Such perplexity is clearly expected by Jacob, otherwise why should he anticipate it in the instructions he gives to his servant on how to dispel it?

The artist of the miniature on fol. 56r is unusual in showing this gesture being made by two fingers instead of one, although the same preference is seen in the drawing of another manuscript which is also probably from the medieval house of St Augustine's, Canterbury, and has also found its present home in the British Library: Royal 6. B. VIII, fols. 1–26. Its decoration Temple associates with that of an Amalarius from St Augustine's that is now Cambridge, Trinity College B. 11. 2,[11] and she believes that it was made at the end of the tenth or beginning of the eleventh century.[12] It is a copy of St Isidore's treatise, *De fide catholica*, which is prefaced by an epistle written by the author to his sister. The epistle begins with a historiated initial on fol. 1v, and it is to this that we wish to direct attention.

It is formed by two gracefully bending figures who outline the initial letter of the first words of address of the writer to his sister, 'Sancte sorori' (pl. XXXIV). The uppermost figure points two fingers to his forehead in the gesture we are discussing, while holding a cross-shaft in his other hand. The lower one looks up to him and gestures expansively towards the commencement of Isidore's epistle with one hand, holding a manuscript with the other. The message of the epistle is that the Old Testament has numerous prophecies of the Nativity, Passion, Death, Resurrection and final vindication of Christ as Judge and King, and that from these the writer intends to select a few examples which, he says, will confirm the Christian in his faith[13] (that is, dispel any lingering doubts) as well as refute the views of the unbeliever. If, then, we interpret the figures in the

rams, thirty milch camels with their colts, and forty kine, and twenty bulls, and twenty she-asses with their ten colts, and he sent out his servants and each of the herds separately before him and said to the servants: "If you meet Esau, my brother, and he should ask you who you are from, or where you want to go, or who owns the things with which you travel, then say that it is from Jacob and he sends it to his lord Esau as a gift."'

[11] See Temple, *Anglo-Saxon Manuscripts*, no. 54, p. 73.   [12] *Ibid.*
[13] The actual words are 'autoritas fidei gratiam firmet'.

light of what has already been argued, we can conclude that the top figure represents the Christian who may have some uncertainties, and the lower one shows him how to resolve them. This will be by reading the words of Isidore to which the lower figure points, which will be substantiated by the quotations from the Old Testament which he clasps to him (the fact that the book is held in a veiled hand certainly indicates that it contains the Holy Word).

In other manuscripts, the gesture is more conventionally represented with one finger only pointing at the face or forehead.

This is true, for example, of a scene in the Sacramentary of Robert of Jumièges (Rouen, Bibliothèque Municipale, Y. 6 (274)), so called because it was given by Robert, when bishop of London from 1044 to 1051, to the house at Jumièges which he had formerly ruled as abbot.

The style of its illustrations associates it with two other manuscripts of the first half of the eleventh century, one the Arenberg Gospels (New York, Pierpont Morgan Library, M 869),[14] which is probably from Christ Church, Canterbury, and the other, the Eadui Psalter, which we shall come to later and which was certainly made there. We might add that, although this will mean comparing paintings with coloured drawings, its 'streamers of colour', if we may borrow an apt phrase of Turner's,[15] have similarities with those in the illustrations of the Harley Psalter which we shall also discuss later, and which, too, was made at Christ Church – probably about the year 1000. All this combines with the fact that Bishop has identified the hand of the main scribe with one that occurs in seven other manuscripts or fragments, three of which are attributable to Canterbury (two specifically to Christ Church),[16] to make us feel reasonably confident that this was itself produced at Christ Church. Its invocation of St Florentinus in the litany for the sick on fol. 207v places it after 1015 since the latter's relics were translated (at Peterborough) in that year, and it has been dated around 1020.

A sacramentary contains the proper prayers for a priest or bishop to recite at masses throughout the liturgical year. This sacramentary, although now missing some leaves, is still sumptuously illuminated with

---

[14] Temple, *Anglo-Saxon Manuscripts*, no. 72.

[15] Backhouse, Turner and Webster, *The Golden Age of Anglo-Saxon Art*, no. 50.

[16] Bishop, 'The Copenhagen Gospel Book', pp. 39–40; and Bishop, *English Caroline Minuscule*, p. xv. See also Ker, *Catalogue of Manuscripts Containing Anglo-Saxon*, no. 377; and Temple, *Anglo-Saxon Manuscripts*, no. 72, p. 90.

four decorated pages and thirteen illustrated ones. Two of these are related to the masses for Christmas and we shall here consider the one that features the Nativity on fol. 32v.[17]

It is dominated by the recumbent figure of the Virgin, whose head is supported by a cushion which is being adjusted by a nimbed woman. The latter is being addressed by an angel so that, in terms of the apocryphal Book of James,[18] she is probably Salome. She appears in Byzantine art and also in other areas of western art, including that of Anglo-Saxon England, as in the Benedictional of St Æthelwold (BL Additional 49598, 15v)[19] and in a particularly attractive carving in walrus ivory which is now Liverpool, Merseyside County Museums, Mayer Collection, M 8060.[20] Below, the Christ child is shown reclining in a gold-framed crib. So far, there is much that is conventional about the iconography of the scene. However, this is far from true of the figure of Joseph. In a tradition that extended from around 600[21] until well into the Gothic period,[22] Joseph was normally represented in scenes of the Nativity with his hand to his face or chin, and so he appears in other examples of Anglo-Saxon art as in the carving we have just referred to, and even in a marginal drawing from Canterbury itself.[23] Yet in the sacramentary, we find a complete departure from this firmly established tradition, for Joseph is now seen pointing a finger at his face (pl. XXXV*a*). This is the Terentian gesture we are discussing and, to my knowledge, it is not found elsewhere in any of the numerous scenes of the Nativity of the medieval period. There is a further feature of the Joseph portrayal which is exceptional, if not unique, namely that he holds a book. The only parallel to this appears to be in a late twelfth-century manuscript painting from lower Saxony

---

[17] There is a colour reproduction of it in Backhouse, Turner and Webster, *The Golden Age of Anglo-Saxon Art*, pl. 50.

[18] Cf. Book of James XX.3; James, *The Apocryphal New Testament*, p. 47.

[19] Beckwith, *Ivory Carvings in Early Medieval England*, pl. 55; and Deshman, *The Benedictional of Æthelwold*, pl. 12 (in colour).

[20] Beckwith, *Ivory Carvings in Early Medieval England*, pl. 56.

[21] See Morey, *Early Christian Art*, fig. 129 (lower left) which reproduces the painting on a pilgrim's souvenir box now in the Museo Sacro of the Vatican and attributed to *c.* 600 (*ibid.*, p. 281).

[22] See the painting by the Erfurt Master (third quarter of the thirteenth century), Schiller, *Ikonographie der christlichen Kunst* I, fig. 183.

[23] Vatican, Reg. lat. 12, 93r (reproduced in Ohlgren, *Anglo-Saxon Textual Illustration*, 3.37). This is the Bury Psalter which we shall discuss below.

that is now in an American collection,[24] but even this is a false parallel. The German painting was clearly designed by a subtle, if not over-subtle, theologian who appears to have taken the unusual step of using the figure of Joseph as a visual metaphor for the Synagogue itself.[25] In contrast to this, the book held by Joseph in our sacramentary has no abstruse significances, although we should mention that it is given prominence both by its size and by the fact that it is bound in gold. In its context, this can only mean that it contains the Word of God: in other words, it is a copy of the Old Testament.

If, now, we return to the signal being made by Joseph, we would argue that here, as elsewhere, it indicates perplexity. According to the apocryphal Book of James we have already quoted, this would not have been out of place for him. It tells us that Joseph was perplexed as to whether to enter Mary in the taxation register as his wife (which would bring him shame) or as his daughter.[26] He was puzzled again when, towards the end of her pregnancy, he saw her now weeping and now laughing,[27] and again, when he could not make up his mind where to take her for her actual delivery.[28] The apocryphal source also speaks of Joseph's earlier bewilderment when he discovered that the woman he had thought a virgin was pregnant,[29] and an account of this was, of course, given in the more orthodox source of St Matthew's gospel (I.18–21). The latter passage was the gospel reading for the Christmas Eve service, so that the puzzlement of Joseph at some stage of the story of Christ's birth would have been in the forefront of the minds of those worshipping at Christmas. However, the perplexity of Joseph in our picture relates to the child already born, and this needs further elucidation.

If we examine the miniature, we shall see that Joseph is visually associated with three focal points in it: the gesture of puzzlement that he gives, the Old Testament bound in gold that he holds in his left hand, and the Christ child on whom he fixes his gaze. From the Christian

---

[24] It is on a single leaf, taken from a Saxon Gospel Book (Trier, Domschatz 142), and now in the Museum of Art, Cleveland, Ohio. Its date is *c.* 1170–90, and it has a picture of the birth of Christ with one of *Ecclesia* above. See Schiller, *Ikonographie der christlichen Kunst* I, fig. 173.

[25] *Ibid.*, p. 84.

[26] Book of James XVII.1; James, *The Apocrypyhal New Testament*, p. 45.

[27] Book of James XVII.2; *ibid.*   [28] Book of James XVII.3; *ibid.*, p. 46.

[29] Book of James XIII.1; *ibid.*, p. 44.

perspective, the birth of the Saviour is of course the fulfilment of the prophecies of the Old Testament, and this fact is given its greatest emphasis during the Christmas services. The epistle for the Vigil of the Nativity on Christmas Eve is thus a passage from St Paul's epistle to the Romans (I.1–6) which speaks of the gospel of Christ 'quod ante promiserat per prophetas suos in scripturis sanctis',[30] and the gradual for this service is taken from Exodus XVI and promises that the glory of the Lord will appear on the morn (vv. 6–7). The masses for Christmas Day itself include not only two readings from Isaiah prognosticating the birth of the Christ child,[31] but also an extract from Paul's epistle to the Hebrews saying that God had spoken through his prophets and was now speaking through his son.[32] Again, the extracts that are read from the psalms are those that prophesy the coming of the Redeemer, one declaring that God's son is begotten this day,[33] another that the Lord is come,[34] and yet another that 'uenit in nomine Domini'.[35] It is in just this context, I would suggest, that this small part of our picture should be interpreted. If Joseph gestures puzzlement here, it is because he is indeed perplexed: perplexed that the great prophecies in the Old Testament he holds should be fulfilled in this small child, who has been born to his own wife in this humblest of dwellings, and to whom he is giving his fullest attention.

The gesture made by Joseph is found again in a scene of a manuscript known as the Tiberius Psalter (BL Cotton Tiberius C. vi).

The pictures of the psalter betray one iconographical association with Canterbury, and this is in the curious representation of the Creation on fol. 7v, in which the Creator is seen with two trumpet-like objects issuing from his mouth (representing the breath of God according to Wormald,[36] and the second person of the Trinity according to Heimann),[37] and where one hand appears holding scales and a pair of dividers. A dove, to signify the Holy Spirit, completes the composition. This has a kinship with miniatures in three earlier manuscripts, all originating in Canterbury –

---

[30] Romans I.2: 'which he [God] had promised long ago through his prophets in the holy Scriptures'.

[31] Isaiah IX.2 and IX.6; introits of second and third mass.

[32] Hebrews I.12; epistle for third mass.   [33] Ps. II.7; introit for first mass.

[34] Ps. XCV.11 and 13; offertory for first mass.

[35] Ps. CXVII.26 ('he comes in the name of the Lord'); gradual for second mass.

[36] Wormald, 'An English Eleventh-Century Psalter with Pictures', p. 8.

[37] Heimann, 'Three Illustrations from the Bury St Edmunds Psalter', p. 52.

the Bury St Edmunds Psalter that we shall come to later (Vatican, Reg. lat. 12, 68v), a bible (BL Royal 1. E. VII, 1v), and the Eadui Gospels (Hanover, Kestner Museum WM XXI[a] 36, 10r). Despite this, the Winchester origin of the Tiberius Psalter seems assured, for Wormald[38] and Bishop[39] concur in the view that there is evidence to demonstrate that it was made there, and on palaeographic grounds it has been assigned to the mid-eleventh century. With this the artistic style agrees, for the bold, if still vigorous, quality of the line signals the approach of Romanesque.

The art-historical importance of the pictures lies in the fact that they are the earliest to survive from the Middle Ages which illustrate the Psalter with full-page depictions of the life of David and of Christ himself (the Middle Ages were imbued with the views of the Fathers, such as Jerome,[40] that the psalms represented the voice not only of David but also of Christ), and thus we have here, as Wormald says, 'the ancestor of a long and illustrious line of illuminated manuscripts, which includes such books as the St Albans Psalter at Hildesheim and the Ingeburg Psalter at Chantilly.'[41] Included among its eleven pictures is one that shows, on fol. 11v, Christ washing the feet of the disciples with the related inscription: 'HIC FECIT IESVS MANDATVM CVM DISCIPVLIS SVIS'. The originality of the scene, particularly in terms of the angel descending with the towel, has been emphasized by Kantorowicz,[42] but our own interest in it is in something quite different: it is in the gesture being made by Peter. He is shown seated, with one foot outstretched in anticipation of the ministrations of his master, who himself kneels before him, with his hands poised forward as he awaits delivery of the towel. In the meantime, the disciple is pointing a rigid forefinger towards his forehead (pl. XXXV*b*). It is our gesture for puzzlement. And very

---

[38] 'An English Eleventh-Century Psalter with Pictures', p. 3. In fact, Wormald is rather cautiously agreeing with the Sisams: see Sisam and Sisam, *The Salisbury Psalter*, pp. 4–5. The points of reference are psalm-divisions and, of the four psalters cited, Wormald says that two are certainly Winchester manuscripts. They are BL Cotton Vitellius E. xviii and Arundel 60.

[39] *English Caroline Minuscule*, no. 27.

[40] *Breuiarium in Psalmos, Prologus*: 'Quamuis Dauid omnes psalmos cantasset ... per titulum intelligitur, in cuius persona cantatur aut in persona Christi, aut in ... persona prophetae' (PL XXVI, 824).

[41] 'An English Eleventh-Century Psalter with Pictures', p. 1.

[42] Kantorowicz, 'The Baptism of the Apostles'.

appropriate it is here. In verses 5 to 10 of chapter XIII of his gospel, the evangelist John describes Peter's state of perplexity at this moment – first enquiring whether his own feet will be washed as well as the others', next refusing to allow it, and then asking for his hands and head to be washed as well. Christ goes further and draws attention to Peter's mystification at a much deeper level when he says, 'quod ego facio, tu nescis modo.'[43] It is hardly an accident, then, that Peter is shown giving the Terentian indicator of bewilderment as Christ prepares to give the same attention to him that he has given to the other disciples. It is a gesture taken up by the Anglo-Saxons, but not, to the best of my knowledge, found elsewhere in contemporary or earlier Christian art.

GRIEF OR SADNESS

We remarked in an earlier chapter[44] that there were many ways of expressing grief in the classical period. Fingering the eye as if to wipe away a tear, covering up the face with one or both hands, or with a garment, tearing the hair or breast, striking the head or lowering it to gaze at the floor, laying the cheek against the hand, placing one hand over the head as if to strike – these were all used as indicators of sadness. Yet to a large extent, actors seem to have opted for the one in which the curved or flat hand is laid near or to the side of the cheek and, as we earlier demonstrated,[45] we find this both in a terracotta of a lamenting figure which survives from as early as the fourth century BC and in our Terence miniatures which derive from an archetype of some 600 years later, and which we exemplify here with a portrayal of the grieving Clinia (pl. XXXVI*a*) which occurs in the illustration to Act III, scene 3 of *Heauton timorumenos*. It is of some significance, then, to see that it is just this way of expressing grief that is used by Anglo-Saxon artists. We shall begin our exemplifications of this by looking at its occurrence in the miniatures of the Canterbury Hexateuch where it is often found in the obvious contexts of deaths and funerals.

Thus, it is displayed by the widow of Enos (pl. XXXVI*b*) as she sits at the foot of his shrouded body in the lowest scene of fol. 10v (Gen. V.11), by the relict of Jared, who takes up the same position in the upper picture

[43] John XIII.7: 'What I do, thou knowest not now.' [44] See above, p. 33.
[45] See above, p. 33.

111

of fol. 11v (Gen. V.20), and by the bereaved wife of Methuselah[46] in the top right-hand part of the miniature on fol. 12r (Gen. V.27). Tamar signals her despondency in the same way as the shrouded body of her husband, Er, is being lifted up nearby (fol. 55v, above) and as his brother, now expected to act as a surrogate spouse, addresses her (Gen. XXXVIII.7–9). Although the shrouding of Cainan's body is, in fact, depicted in an adjacent frame, it is not his widow who is shown in sorrow on fol. 11r (upper register), but the person being informed of his death who is presumably his son and heir, Mahalaleel (Gen. V.15–17).[47]

Enoch did not die, but was transported to heaven as we see represented in the lower part of fol. 11v (Gen. V.24). Nonetheless, there is a woman grieving in the adjacent compartment, in a scene which presumably represents the news of the passing of Enoch being reported to his son, Methuselah, unless it represents some earlier incident in Enoch's life (in which case the figure seated next to the woman would be Enoch himself, not Methuselah). The mourning for Jacob is given as much weight in the illustrations as in the Latin and Old English accounts, and is spread over five of the unfinished pictures. In the first (fol. 71r, above), all the sons are seen giving the now familiar Terentian signal for grief as they mourn their father while he is being shrouded (Gen. L.3), and there follows in the next picture (fol. 71r, below) the intercession with Pharaoh for permission to carry out the dead man's wishes (Gen. L.4–6). This is granted so that his body can be transported to the land of Canaan, which event is illustrated just below the intercession scene (Gen. L.7–9). The cortège, now in carriages, continues at the top of the next page, and the main obsequies, with the great mourning and lamentations referred to in verses 10 and 11 of the biblical account, take place lower down where conspicuous use is made of the gesture we are discussing. It is again called upon to express distress in the final scene (fol. 72r, above) where the body is blessed and lowered down (Gen. L.12–13). The same gesture is used to symbolize the mourning of the people at the death of Aaron, which is depicted in the unfinished picture at the top of fol. 123r and described in Numbers XX.29, and it features very prominently in the lamentations for the loss of Moses (pl. XXXVII) in the full-page picture of his final time on earth that we find on fol. 139v (Deut. XXXIV.8).

In an unfinished picture in the lowest register of fol. 119r, the Israelites

---

[46] The gesture here is not well defined.   [47] The gesture here is not well defined.

are shown signalling their grief in the same manner, this time both for their sins and also for the deaths that the Lord has inflicted on those of their number who have been complaining about him (Num. XIV.39). However, they do not have recourse to this indication of sadness simply on occasions of what we might call ritual mourning. They find it an equally apt indicator of grief of a more private sort and this can, of course, occur at various degrees of intensity.

As he disconsolately walks away from the scene of Noah blessing his two brothers on fol. 18r (above), Ham finds this an appropriate gesture to express the distress he feels at the curse that his father has instead laid on his head for failing to help him when he lay in his drunken stupor (Gen. IX.25–7). And in the same way, in the upper miniature on fol. 28r, Hagar can call on the same gesture to indicate her state of dejection at the way she has been ill-treated by her mistress, Sarah. Isaac can make use of it, too, to indicate in one place (fol. 41v) how disconsolate he is to be reminded of the onset of death by old age and blindness (Gen. XXVII.1), and in another (fol. 42v), how saddened he is by the realisation that he has been deceived into depriving his elder son of his rightful blessing (pl. XXXVIII*a*). Jacob employs it on fol. 46r (above) to show how aggrieved he feels towards his father-in-law for his unfair treatment which, in the event, forces him to pack up all his possessions and depart (Gen. XXXI.5–7). And much later (fol. 54v, lower area), he utilizes it again to express the total heartbreak he feels at being shown apparently irrefutable evidence of the death of his favourite son, Joseph (pl. XXXVIII*b*). His desolation of heart continues to be signalled on the next folio (top register) where the related text tells us that his grief could not be assuaged by all the efforts of his remaining sons and that he is determined to carry his mourning down with him even to hell itself (Gen. XXXVII.34–5). We may here note that, although (v. 34) he expresses his anguish by tearing his clothes and putting on sackcloth according to both the Latin ('Scissisque vestibus, indutus est cilicio') and the Old English ('He totær hys reaf 7 scrydde hyne mid hæran'),[48] the Anglo-Saxon artist has preferred to keep to the Terentian form of expression with which he was familiar. And in the meantime (middle register of the same folio), it proves to be a useful indicator of the grief that Joseph himself feels at being sold to an Egyptian eunuch (Gen. XXXVII.36).

---

[48] Crawford, *Heptateuch*, p. 174.

On fol. 76r, Moses calls upon this gesture to express his anxiety at learning that his murder of an Egyptian is now a matter of common knowledge – in fact, his concern is such that he finds it expedient to flee the country (Exod. II.15). Then, on fol. 108v (top left), Aaron can turn to it to express the grief he feels as he witnesses the destruction by fire of his sons Nadab and Abihu (Levit. X.1–3).

We could offer yet more examples to support our view that the gesture for grief of the Roman stage was adopted as a useful formula by the artists of the Hexateuch, but these twenty-two should be sufficient to make our point. I may add, by way of parenthesis, that in an earlier publication, I gave some emphasis to the originality of the Anglo-Saxon miniaturists of this manuscript,[49] and the findings I have recounted above will go some way to reinforcing this, since the particular gesture for grief that we have described here is not one used in early Christian or post-classical art.

It did, however, appear in other Anglo-Saxon manuscripts, one of them, like the Hexateuch, being chiefly celebrated for its vernacular text which was once attributed to the poet Cædmon whom Bede praised so fulsomely. The manuscript is now Oxford, Bodleian Library, Junius 11. It contains the Old English poems *Genesis*, *Exodus*, *Daniel* and *Christ and Satan*, and is, in fact, a composite work, for it includes within *Genesis* an interpolated translation from the Old Saxon, known as *Genesis B*. Gollancz, indeed, believed that codicological evidence indicated that it was in this actual manuscript that the interpolation first took place,[50] although subsequent scholarship has cast doubt on this.[51] On p. 2 is a small medallion profile-bust inscribed 'Ælfwine', and this led Gollancz to associate the manuscript with the Winchester house of Newminster, since a monk of that name became abbot there in 1031.[52] However, the name is not an unusual one, and it now appears more likely that the manuscript was made at Christ Church, Canterbury.[53] It seems at least to have been there in the Middle Ages, for many years ago M. R. James pointed out

---

[49] Dodwell and Clemoes, *The Old English Illustrated Hexateuch*, pp. 65–73.

[50] Gollancz, *The Cædmon Manuscript*, p. liii. His view is repeated by Temple, *Anglo-Saxon Manuscripts*, p. 76.

[51] See Raw, 'The Construction of Oxford, Bodleian Library, Junius 11', pp. 193–5; and Doane, *The Saxon Genesis*, p. 34.

[52] Gollancz, *The Cædmon Manuscript*, pp. xxxv–xxxvi.

[53] Lucas has argued that Junius 11 was produced at Malmesbury, but this has been rejected by Thomson. See Lucas, 'MS Junius 11 and Malmesbury', esp. pp. 213–20;

that it is probably the 'Genesis Anglice depicta', no. 304 of Prior Eastry's fourteenth-century catalogue of the books there (it is itself inscribed 'Genesis in anglico' on p. ii).[54] Pächt and Alexander have drawn our attention to the fact that the second of its artists worked on a Prudentius manuscript (CCCC 23)[55] which is attributed to Christ Church on stylistic grounds.[56] Its date, as suggested both by Ker and by Pächt and Alexander, is around the year 1000.[57]

The Junius manuscript (as it is commonly known), like the Hexateuch, has a cycle of illustrations of the Old Testament, although this is very different from the one produced in the neighbouring house, and it is incomplete, with numerous spaces at the end left blank for illustrations that were never inserted. If we exclude two unfinished drawings added in the twelfth century and drawings in hard point of uncertain date,[58] we can say that the cycle concludes with an illustration of Abraham leading his tribe towards Egypt (Gen. XII.10). The illustrations are variously full- and part-page, and, with the exception of the fully painted figure of the Almighty within one illustration (on p. 11), take the form of coloured line-drawings with occasional washes of colour.

A particularly powerful part of the narrative of *Genesis* is that between lines 235 and 851 where we are given an account of the Fall of Man. The poet has enhanced its drama by a very full narration of the fall of Satan which led to this. Once the most favoured of the angels, his pride led him to revolt against his maker and, as a result, he had been hurled into the abyss of hell. The poet describes his envy of Adam who has been given a place in the cosmos which, in his (Satan's) view, should belong to himself, and also his rancour towards God, and how these together led him to

and Thomson, 'Identifiable Books from the Pre-Conquest Library of Malmesbury Abbey', pp. 16–18.

[54] James, *Ancient Libraries*, pp. 51 and 509.

[55] Pächt and Alexander, *Illuminated Manuscripts in the Bodleian Library Oxford* III, 5, no. 34.

[56] Temple, *Anglo-Saxon Manuscripts*, no. 48, p. 70; and see also the full account of the manuscript in Budny, *Insular, Anglo-Saxon, and Early Anglo-Norman Manuscript Art* I, no. 24.

[57] Ker, *Catalogue of Manuscripts Containing Anglo-Saxon*, no. 334; Pächt and Alexander, as note 55. Others have seen Viking influence in aspects of the decoration, and have favoured a date within the reign of Cnut, *c.* 1025; see, for example, Doane, *Genesis A*, p. 18.

[58] See Ohlgren, 'Five New Drawings'.

agree a plan to ensnare the former and thereby thwart the will of the latter. A very full recital is given of the scenes of the subsequent temptations of Adam and Eve, and once the devil's scheme has been accomplished, the theme is very much that of anguish on earth. It is on this that we wish to focus.

We are soon told that:

> Sorgedon ba twa,
> Adam and Eue,   and him oft betuh
> gnornword gengdon;[59]

that:

> Þæt wif gnornode,
> hof hreowigmod;[60]

that:

> him higesorga
> burnon on breostum;[61]

that:

> Þa hie fela spræcon
> sorhworda somed,   sinhiwan twa;[62]

that Adam tells Eve:

> Nu wit hreowige magon
> sorgian for þis siðe;[63]

and that both uttered words of bitter regret, Adam against Eve and Eve against herself for her own action.[64]

The prominence that the poet gives to the grief of the devil's victims is emphatically taken up by the illustrator, who signifies it no less than eight times in the brief space of six pages. Within the full-page setting

---

[59] *Genesis* 765b–767a (Krapp, *The Junius Manuscript*, p. 26): 'Adam and Eve both grieved, and sad words often passed between them'.

[60] *Genesis* 770b–771a (*ibid.*, p. 26): 'The woman grieved and sorrowfully lamented'.

[61] *Genesis* 776b–777a (*ibid.*, p. 26): 'Heart-sorrow burned in their breasts'.

[62] *Genesis* 788b–789b (*ibid.*, p. 27): 'Many words of grief they exchanged, the two of them'.

[63] *Genesis* 799b–800a (*ibid.*, p. 27): 'Now in grief we may sorrow for this undertaking'.

[64] *Genesis* 810–26 (*ibid.*, pp. 27–8).

on p. 34,[65] we see (above) Adam and Eve looking towards one another as they indicate their sorrow (pl. XXXIX*a*), and (below) each still registering sadness as they stand gazing in each other's direction. In the latter picture, they are seen trying to conceal themselves behind trees within a woodland, and endeavouring to hide their private shame with foliage (cf. *Genesis* 838–40a and 845–6). In a full-page miniature on p. 36,[66] at a time when the success of the devil's mission is being reported in hell in a scene below, they display by their gestures (pl. XXXIX*b*) that on earth their woefulness continues, and on p. 39[67] the drawing represents the continuance of their heartache as they sit under trees well away from each other:

> Hwurfon hie ba twa,
> togendon gnorngende   on þone grenan weald,
> sæton onsundran.[68]

Now, it is notable that, during the course of the recital of their miseries and woes, the artist has decided that he has need of only one gesture to signify their state of wretchedness. This is the one for grief on which we are focusing. Further, the whole of this particular passage is the one translated from the Old Saxon and inserted into the text, so that these illustrations were presumably created expressly for this composite text, whether that text first appeared in this very manuscript (as Gollancz believed) or in an Anglo-Saxon exemplar from which it may have been copied (as more recent scholarship has concluded). In other words, the illustrations are Anglo-Saxon creations, and the gestures in them could not have been taken over from any pre-existing or conventional model.[69] Like other Terentian gestures, this one has simply become an Anglo-Saxon one.

It occurs again in a manuscript more securely attributed to Canterbury. This is the earliest of the three Canterbury copies of the celebrated Utrecht Psalter (Utrecht, Bibliotheek der Rijksuniversiteit,

[65] Ohlgren, *Anglo-Saxon Textual Illustration*, 16.17.
[66] *Ibid.*, 16.18.   [67] *Ibid.*, 16.19.
[68] *Genesis* 840b–842a (Krapp, *The Junius Manuscript*, p. 28): 'They both turned and went grieving into the green grove and sat down apart from each other.'
[69] Raw's attempts ('The Probable Derivation of Most of the Illustrations in Junius 11', pp. 137–42) to associate some aspects of this area of the illustrations with early Christian/Carolingian art seem to me unpersuasive.

32)[70] which itself originated at Reims; the copy is known as the Harley Psalter and is BL Harley 603.

Both Wormald[71] and Temple[72] attribute it to the early eleventh century, while Backhouse would give slightly more definition to the date-bracket by placing the manuscript in the century's second or third decade.[73] (Her suggestion that the episcopal figure shown prostrating himself before Christ in the *Beatus* initial on fol. 2r is Æthelnoth, a former dean of Christ Church who was made archbishop of Canterbury in 1020, is especially interesting.)[74] The illustrations of the Utrecht Psalter are usually detailed and literal, and it was originally intended that the drawings of the Harley Psalter should be faithful copies of them except that their line should be in varied colours of red, green, sepia and blue instead of the simple bistre of the originals. This was indeed achieved by the initial team of illuminators who numbered four in all,[75] although they fell far short of completing their work which, in the event, had even to be continued in the twelfth century. Their endeavours were first resumed in the second quarter of the eleventh century by two miniaturists[76] who, however, took little or no notice of the Utrecht illustrations and simply went their own way. It is a group of the drawings of the second of these two artists, on fols. 67v, 70r and 72v, that we should like to consider here. These drawings are not simply copies of those in the Utrecht Psalter and can be fairly described as Anglo-Saxon originals.

[70] Although it is far from being the best, the most accessible facsimile of the manuscript is still DeWald, *The Illustrations of the Utrecht Psalter*.

[71] Wormald, *English Drawings*, p. 69.

[72] Temple, *Anglo-Saxon Manuscripts*, no. 64. On p. 81, she says, like Wormald, that it is early eleventh-century. On p. 82, she suggests a date of *c.* 1000 or soon after.

[73] Backhouse, Turner and Webster, *The Golden Age of Anglo-Saxon Art*, no. 59, p. 75.

[74] *Ibid.*

[75] This is the view of Wormald (*English Drawings*, p. 70), who labels the hands A, B, C and D, and identifies the folios on which their work is seen. Backhouse, who has also made a detailed study of the manuscript, thinks that there are three hands where Wormald has four: see Backhouse, 'The Making of the Harley Psalter'; and Backhouse, Turner and Webster, *The Golden Age of Anglo-Saxon Art*, p. 75. The final part of the manuscript following Ps. CXLIII.12 has been lost.

[76] Wormald (as last note) refers to these as hands E and F. He says that hand E added drawings unrelated to the text on blank spaces on fols. 1r, 15r, 15v, 53r, 58v, 61r, 61v, 62v, 67r, 70r, 70v and 72v, and that hand F illustrated fols. 58r–73v. It is hand F that concerns us here. As Wormald notes, his illustrations 'are not copied from the Utrecht Psalter, though individual details are'.

The first of them, on the lower part of the folio, illustrates the very brief Psalm CXXX.[77] In it, the psalmist says that, like a weaned child, he has now found humility, and the picture includes a representation of a child already weaned from its mother. There is also represented a small group of the Israelites (pl. XL*a*), on whose behalf the psalmist has been speaking, who are expressing their grief for the lack of a proper docility in the past which the verses seem to imply. One point to be made is that they are using the Terentian formula to indicate their sorrow. Another is that the miniature as a whole is quite different from the one in the Utrecht Psalter. There (on fol. 74v) the psalmist is pictured in the centre raising his arms to God, who is in a mandorla above and accompanied by angels, then there is a group of armed Israelites on the right and of unarmed ones on the left, and also a woman with a child at her breast below.

Our second example is an illustration of Psalm CXXXVI.[78] The Utrecht artist had pictured this very fulsomely indeed with the intention of missing no incident and, as a result, his scene on fol. 77r is crowded with more than fifty figures. They portray a veritable army besieging and destroying the cities of Edom and Babylon (vv. 7–9), Christ with disciples on a hillock, the psalmist and others appealing to heaven, a small group before a tabernacle, and the Israelites meditating on their fate as a group of Babylonians urge them to sing their songs. The Harley artist, on the other hand, has only interested himself in the plight of the Israelites. He shows them in their desolation as they are being addressed – 'Super flumina Babylonis illic sedimus et fleuimus, cum recordaremur Sion'[79] – and depicts them mourning by the river-side, their harps hung up in the background – 'Quomodo cantabimus canticum Domini in terra aliena?'[80] If, within the small group of lamenting figures, we focus attention on the two central ones (pl. XL*b*), we shall see that they are expressing their grief by the Terentian gesture we have described.

The same gesture is called on to indicate sadness in the upper picture of fol. 72v to Psalm CXLI.[81] This the Utrecht Psalter (fol. 79v) illustrates as follows. It shows a central figure appealing to Christ (himself grouped

---

[77] Ohlgren, *Anglo-Saxon Textual Illustration*, 2.90.   [78] *Ibid.*, 2.95.

[79] Ps. CXXXVI.1: 'By the rivers of Babylon, there we sat down, yea we wept, when we remembered Zion'.

[80] Ps. CXXXVI.4: 'How shall we sing the Lord's song in a strange land?'

[81] Ohlgren, *Anglo-Saxon Textual Illustration*, 2.100.

with other figures) and at the same time pointing to the net being prepared for him. A number of his persecutors are represented on the left, and groups of the righteous by the rivers of Paradise on the right. The Harley picture also has persecutors and the righteous, as the text suggests (vv. 3–5 and 8), but the interpretations are somewhat different and, furthermore, the central figure is now being rescued from a pit by a descending angel. The real point, however, is that the Harley Psalter makes a significant addition: it is of the psalmist expressing his personal feelings. The basic message of the psalm is the anguish of the writer, who cries out that, because of the insuperable problems confronting him, his spirit has failed (v. 4), and that because of the assaults of persecutors stronger than himself, he has been brought low (v. 7); only God can now help him. The portrayal of him in the lower part of the composition certainly gives eloquent expression to this mood of someone lost in grief (pl. XLI*a*), and this is achieved by the use of our present gesture.

The view of Backhouse is that the style of the last artist is 'very close' to that of a 'slightly later' psalter now in Rome (Vatican, Reg. lat. 12).[82] Entries in its calendar make it clear that it was produced for Bury St Edmunds, but the stylistic and iconographic evidence of its pictures is equally emphatic in showing that it was made at Christ Church, Canterbury. It is usually dated to the second quarter of the eleventh century. Although made at about the same time and in the same centre as the Harley Psalter, its illustrations are usually quite dissimilar,[83] and this is for two reasons: because they take the form of marginal drawings and because their content tends to be different. It is the illustration to Psalm VII that will interest us here.

David begins the psalm by making a strong appeal to God for his protection: 'Saluum me fac ex omnibus persequentibus me, et libera me, ne quando rapiat ut leo animam meam.'[84] He then goes on to comfort himself with thoughts of the justice and strength of the Lord who has stored up punishments for the unrepentant: 'Arcum suum tetendit, et parauit illum.'[85] The response of the miniaturist has been to show in the

---

[82] Backhouse, Turner and Webster, *The Golden Age of Anglo-Saxon Art*, p. 75.

[83] In fact, the artist has excerpted some iconographic details from the Utrecht Psalter, but such borrowings are few.

[84] Ps. VII.2–3: 'Save me from all that persecute me, and deliver me, lest at any time he seize upon my soul like a lion.'

[85] Ps. VII.13: 'He hath stretched his bow and made it ready.'

lower right-hand corner of the relevant folio (24v) a demonic figure with bent bow.[86] In it he holds an arrow which is being directed towards a woman seated at the top of the adjacent page (25r),[87] this being part of the same picture-space when the book is opened up. And there the arrow is seen actually piercing her, for she represents the ungodly for whom God's punishment is reserved. As such, she holds a pot labelled with two words of verse 14 which says that God has made ready for the impious the vessels of death, 'vasa mortis'. The flames leaping from the pot are in response to the words of verse 14, 'sagittas suas ardentibus effecit',[88] an association between fire and the punishment of the evil-doer that is seen in other parts of the bible. The progeny of the unrighteous, according to the psalmist, will be injustice, sorrow and iniquity – 'Ecce parturiit iniustitiam; concepit dolorem, et peperit iniquitatem' (v. 15) – and, if the heads of the newly-born vices that peer out from the woman's bosom number eight instead of three, this, according to Heimann,[89] is because of influences from a copy of Prudentius' *Psychomachia* where a depiction of Avaritia is similar to the figure here and a marginal comment tells us that 'multitudinem vitiorum Avaritia nigro lacte nutrit'.[90] We happen to know that Christ Church probably had two illustrated copies of Prudentius at the time,[91] and the further fact that the vices there are in female form may explain why the artist of the Bury Psalter also presents his personification of the unrighteous as a woman. She is herself in a state of woe (pl. XLI*b*), and although two particular references in the text do associate her with sadness – verse 15, quoted above, speaks of her conceiving sorrow, and verse 17 talks of the sorrow that is turned back upon her head: 'convertetur dolor eius in caput eius' – her gesture here probably indicates the more general state of anguish of the ungodly when they recall their past sins and consider their future punishment. It is a

---

[86] Ohlgren, *Anglo-Saxon Textual Illustration*, 3.4.   [87] *Ibid.*, 3.5.

[88] 'He hath made his arrows for them that burn'.

[89] Heimann, 'Three Illustrations from the Bury St Edmunds Psalter', p. 52.

[90] 'Avarice suckles a multitude of vices with black milk'.

[91] CCCC 23 (Temple, *Anglo-Saxon Manuscripts*, no. 48) and BL Cotton Cleopatra C. viii (*ibid.*, no. 49). The Corpus manuscript had reached Malmesbury by the mid-eleventh century. For the relevant illustrations in the two manuscripts, see Budny, *Insular, Anglo-Saxon, and Early Anglo-Norman Manuscript Art* II, pl. 262; and Ohlgren, *Anglo-Saxon Textual Illustration*, 15.35.

state expressed with great eloquence in this noble drawing which makes use of a modified form of the Terentian gesture for grief.

APPROVAL OR ACQUIESCENCE

The Harley and the Bury Psalters differ from each other in their illustrations, but there is another Canterbury manuscript whose pictures offer a complete contrast to them both. It is the Eadui Psalter (BL Arundel 155), and it brings to our attention another gesture that the Anglo-Saxons borrowed from the Terence repertory. It is one which needs some clarification.

We saw in our last chapter that the gesture for agreement, or acquiescence, consisted of curving the thumb and forefinger around until they touched each other, and as such it was represented in the miniatures of the Vatican and Paris manuscripts. However, as we remarked earlier,[92] there was a deviation from this in the pictures of another Carolingian manuscript, the one in Milan: Biblioteca Ambrosiana, S.P. 4 bis. There, in his illustration to Act IV, scene 5 of *Eunuchus*, the artist caused Pythias to replace the forefinger with the third finger in making this gesture (pl. XLII*a*);[93] and in the illustration to Act III, scene 3 of *Heauton timorumenos*, the slave Syrus replaces the forefinger with the second finger as he addresses his master Chremes (pl. XLII*b*).[94] In the latter case, the artist even permitted a gap between the relevant finger and the thumb, and it is this much less familiar form of the gesture that the Anglo-Saxons adopted, as we can see in their illustrations of the Eadui Psalter.

This psalter is so called after the name of the scribe, who has been identified as the one who copied out the Eadui Gospels in which he gives his name.[95] He is known to have been the chief scribe of Christ Church, Canterbury,[96] and this tells us immediately that the psalter was written

---

[92] See above, p. 39 n. 26.   [93] 8v, J&M I, no. 252.

[94] 36v, J&M I, no. 385.   [95] Hanover, Kestner Museum WM XXIᵃ 36.

[96] Apart from in this Hanover codex, Bishop (*English Caroline Minuscule*, p. 22) claims to identify Eadui's hand in ten other manuscripts or documents, namely: Cambridge, Gonville and Caius College 732/754 (a leaf from a service book); Florence, Biblioteca Medicea Laurenziana, Plut. XVII. 20; BL Add. 34890, Arundel 155 (to fol. 191), Cotton Vespasian A. i (part II), Harley 603, fols. 28–49, Royal 1. D. IX, 44v, and Stowe Charters 2 and 38; and York, Chapter Library, Add. 1, fol. 23. For a recent

there, a fact which would, in any case, have been indicated by the calendar which is a Christ Church one and which further points to the date of the manuscript. Its inclusion of the name of St Ælfheah shows that it was written after 1012, the year in which he was martyred by the Danes, and its original omission of any reference to the translation of his relics to Canterbury in 1023 would argue for a date before then. The manuscript is very handsome, its most impressive miniature being the one on fol. 133r after the end of the psalms and before the beginning of the canticles (pl. XLIII).[97] The fact that this, the only full-page picture in the psalter, is of St Benedict may perhaps seem curious until we recall the way in which his Rule and the psalms were so closely intertwined. He himself gives no less than sixty-one quotations from the psalms in the course of his Rule, which itself makes the singing of psalms an essential part of the monastic services, the monks being required to sing all of them during the course of each week and in a specified daily order. As well as in this manuscript, a visual association between the Benedictines and the psalter is to be seen in the Bury Psalter where one monk appears as its scribe in the *Beatus* initial on fol. 21r[98] and another is shown on fol. 37v prostrating himself before a representation of Christ with a book open at the first words of the psalm below: 'Ad te, Domine, leuaui an[imam meam]'.[99]

We have earlier glancingly referred to the fact that the Anglo-Saxon miniaturists were able to differentiate between the relative importance of the characters they were depicting by the use of body-colour and of line, and we see a good example of this here, except that St Benedict is given prominence more by gold than by colour. Indeed, this endows him with such resplendence that, combined as it is with his squarely placed stance facing the spectator, he takes on something of the unapproachable aura of

assessment of Eadui's career and influence, see Dumville, *English Caroline Script and Monastic History*, pp. 120–40.

Boutemy has, without comment, published in his article 'Two Obituaries of Christ Church, Canterbury' an obituary which reads 'Obiit Eadwius sacerdos et monachus'. It is on a flyleaf (p. 297) at the end of London, Lambeth Palace Library, 430, and Boutemy believes that it was written *c.* 1100.

[97] There is a colour plate of the full illustration in Backhouse, Turner and Webster, *The Golden Age of Anglo-Saxon Art*, pl. 57, and a black-and-white one in Temple, *Anglo-Saxon Manuscripts*, pl. 213.

[98] Ohlgren, *Anglo-Saxon Textual Illustration*, 3.1.   [99] *Ibid.*, 3.14.

an icon. This is very different from the impression given by the monks swaying towards him, who are imbued with a refreshing buoyancy by the delicacy of their lightly coloured line.

One message being given by this illustration is of the monks' veneration for their founder, which is indicated by the very opulence with which he is portrayed, but its main purport is not this. It is to show that they are carrying out his Rule, and a copy of the latter is, in fact, being offered to him by the foremost of their number.

It is open at its first words – 'Ausculta, O fili, praecepta [magistri]'[100] – and the miniature incorporates two particular references to its text. One is the description around the saint's halo of him being their father,[101] a term he applies to himself immediately after the exhortation we have just quoted,[102] and the other is the inscription 'TIMOR DEI', the words of Psalm XXXIII.12 which he himself quotes when he tells would-be monks in an early part of his Rule to come and he will teach them fear of the Lord: 'timorem Domini docebo uos.'[103] In the sky above, a hand holds a lengthy inscribed streamer (a Canterbury characteristic), one end of which descends to touch the saint's halo while the other reaches down to the heads of his monks on the right. It gives the appearance of associating the two, and this, indeed, is its purpose as we shall see if we examine the two messages on it.

The first carries a quotation from Christ's pronouncement to his disciples: 'Qui uos audit, me audit.'[104] This is twice used by St Benedict in chapter V of his Rule to reinforce his general insistence on the need for obedience to those in authority since, he argues, 'oboedientia, quae maioribus praebetur, deo exhibetur.'[105] The second message is also concerned with the need for obedience and is a quotation from St Paul's admonition to the Hebrews (XIII.17) to obey their superiors: 'Obedite praepositis uestris.' Now this call to obedience was of great importance to St Benedict. At the very beginning of his Rule, he exhorts those who

---

[100] Cf. Hanslik, *Benedicti Regula*, p. 1: 'Listen, O my son, to the precepts [of thy Master]'.
[101] 'BENEDICTUS PATER MONACHORUM'.
[102] Cf. Hanslik, *Benedicti Regula*, p. 1: 'admonitionem pii *patris* libenter excipe [my italics].'
[103] This is, of course, in the Prologue; cf. *ibid.*, p. 3.
[104] Luke X.16: 'He that heareth you, heareth me.'
[105] Hanslik, *Benedicti Regula*, p. 40: 'the obedience which is given to superiors is given to God.'